"*Ministry Mantras* should be requir[illegible] a small book, it's packed with one big idea—[illegible] looked ways to shape a church's culture lies i[illegible]hrases. As you read this book, get ready to ha[illegible] ignited!"

Derek Cooper, associate professor of world Christian history, Biblical Theological Seminary

"A mantra that I live and lead by is 'words shape imagination.' In *Ministry Mantras*, J.R. Briggs and Bob Hyatt bring their wisdom to bear on how compelling turns of phrase can cultivate kingdom culture. By inviting faith communities to provoke imagination through the use of mantras, they offer one way to help folks internalize grace-filled values and externalize the way of Jesus. Churches and individuals alike will find mantras to live by in this book. I can't recommend it enough!"

Kurt Willems, pastor, Pangea, Seattle; writer, curator, The Paulcast

"This book is a gem! Bob and J.R. translate stories from the trenches of ministry into ridiculously practical principles that are insanely sticky for ministry. These mantras will get stuck in the heads of leaders and the vernaculars of teams. If you are looking for a resource to unite your team around a common way of living and talking about leadership, you've found it!"

Alan Briggs, church planting catalyst, author of *Staying Is the New Going*

"Contemporary ministry has become industrialized. Today we have reduced the mystery of God's working in the world to simple, mechanical formulas and we assume that making disciples is no different than manufacturing widgets: it's all about having the right processes. This often gets expressed in quick-fix, turnkey solutions to any ministry challenge. Unfortunately, the bite-sized morsels of leadership advice that dominate ministry today rarely contain any genuine thoughtfulness, let alone biblical wisdom. That's what makes Briggs and Hyatt so remarkable. They satisfy our cultural desire for the simple without succumbing to the simplistic. Their mantras are short and memorable but they have deep roots in Scripture, tradition and the hard-won wisdom of saints. That makes *Ministry Mantras* a rare book with equal measures of depth and usefulness."

Skye Jethani, author of *With*, cohost, *The Phil Vischer Podcast*

"*Ministry Mantras* is a welcomed water stop in the marathon that is ministry. Unpacking their tough, to-the-point, pithy sayings with real-life and biblical illustrations, Briggs and Hyatt serve a read that is not only refreshing but refueling when facing the ups and downs, celebrations, and challenges of being on God's mission. Whether you take a sip here and there or take it all in during one sitting, you'll find these powerful words resonating in your heart, mind and soul long after the pages have been turned."

Kris Beckert, church planter and mission strategist, Fresh Expressions US

"*Ministry Mantras* is a collection of invaluable insights on leadership and community that have been worked out in the language and the laboratory of the local church. Briggs and Hyatt have curated dozens of memorable sayings that are profound and portable. They are seeds for life and leadership, simple sayings that contain incredible impact. This book will be a well-worn field guide for the wordsmiths, language leaders and cultural creators in the kingdom."

Jared Mackey, pastor, The Sacred Grace, Denver

"J.R. Briggs and Bob Hyatt have given us a gift—a valuable compass complete with instructions. This book is a must-have for any servant, pastor or leader who is passionate about leading their church to the center of Jesus' heart."

Mark E. Strong, lead pastor, Life Change Church, author of *Divine Merger*

"Leaders are cultural architects. If you want to create a missional culture, read this book. J.R. and Bob understand that central to any culture is language. Words shape and form us. Words bring life and death. J.R. and Bob have freshly inspired me to consider the ministry mantras that I need to speak and embody to cultivate the church as movement. For words create worlds and those worlds recreate us."

JR Woodward, national director, V3 Church Planting Movement,
author of *Creating a Missional Culture*, coauthor of *The Church as Movement*

"According to leadership guru Edwin Friedman, leaders are those who describe reality without blame. But ministry rarely allows the space needed to shape words that describe reality well—which is why we need a resource like *Ministry Mantras*, whose simple yet deeply scriptural and practical proverbs help us describe—and shape—reality for our communities. These are not random, pithy sayings, but a holistic, healthy vision of ministry expressed in succinct, everyday language, ready to be shared and repeated. And lived."

Mandy Smith, lead pastor, University Christian Church,
author of *The Vulnerable Pastor*

"Jesus did pithy—so well that people remembered so much of what he said. His brilliance was illuminated by the fact that he always chose to incarnate truth in the words and language of real, everyday people. In short, God spoke our language; he never spoke his own. *Ministry Mantras* reveals a similar commitment—a commitment to bearing the truths of ministry for real people. I commend this book heartily, knowing that it will, like Jesus, offer truths that we can actually remember and use in our lives."

A. J. Swoboda, pastor, professor,
author of *The Dusty Ones* and *Introducing Evangelical Ecotheology*

MINISTRY MANTRAS

LANGUAGE FOR CULTIVATING KINGDOM CULTURE

J.R. BRIGGS / BOB HYATT

Foreword by Leonard Sweet

An imprint of InterVarsity Press
Downers Grove, Illinois

InterVarsity Press
P.O. Box 1400, Downers Grove, IL 60515-1426
ivpress.com
email@ivpress.com

InterVarsity Press® is the book-publishing division of InterVarsity Christian Fellowship/USA®, a movement of students and faculty active on campus at hundreds of universities, colleges and schools of nursing in the United States of America, and a member movement of the International Fellowship of Evangelical Students. For information about local and regional activities, visit intervarsity.org.

While any stories in this book are true, some names and identifying information may have been changed to protect the privacy of individuals.

Published in association with the literary agency of Wolgemuth & Associates.

Cover design: Cindy Kiple
Interior design: Jeanna Wiggins
Images: © rolandtopor/iStockphoto

ISBN 978-0-8308-4136-3 (print)
ISBN 978-0-8308-9186-3 (digital)

Printed in the United States of America ♾

As a member of the Green Press Initiative, InterVarsity Press is committed to protecting the environment and to the responsible use of natural resources. To learn more, visit greenpressinitiative.org.

Library of Congress Cataloging-in-Publication Data
A catalog record for this book is available from the Library of Congress.

P *25 24 23 22 21 20 19 18 17 16 15 14 13 12 11 10 9 8 7 6 5 4 3 2 1*
Y *34 33 32 31 30 29 28 27 26 25 24 23 22 21 20 19 18 17 16*

To Chris Backert

Jesus follower. Kingdom pioneer.
Colleague. Friend. Brother.

CONTENTS

Section Four: Ministry

Section Five: Pastoral Care

Section Six: Leadership Development

Section Seven: Opportunities

FOREWORD

The New Power Outfit

Leonard Sweet

Trial lawyers are now taught that the dark blue suit, white shirt, and red tie are not enough. When you want jurors to focus on you, wear that. But when you are in a direct examination of your client or expert, a better choice is softer earth tones.

But the major ingredient in the new power outfit for trial lawyers is a visual metaphor. Never address a jury without being dressed in some form of visualization. Trial attorneys are now being instructed to never appear before a jury "naked"—that is, without a metaphor—whether that metaphor is your body, or a prop, or something as simple as taking a jelly doughnut out of a bag and crushing it in front of the jury so that the jelly squirts out and stains your suit. You illustrate points. You animate narratives. So crushing a jelly doughnut will show the greatest skeptic how the disks that separate the vertebrae in the spine are just like jelly doughnuts where the nucleus (jelly) can ooze onto your nerves (your tie and shirt) and ruin your life (outfit).

J.R. Briggs and Bob Hyatt have written a book that needs to be read not only by preachers or communicators, but also by everyone growing a deep and wide faith. If language influences the ways in which we view things, metaphors do even more: they shape the ways we understand. Philosopher Nelson Goodman says that images are more than "world mirroring"—they are ways of "worldmaking."[1]

Metaphor is metamorphosis, and our metaphors metamorph our future. More than inform our faith, metaphors *form* our faith, so choose your metaphors carefully. At the heart of every narrative is a metaphor. Metaphors do the heavy lifting in thinking, and to change people's minds is to change or reframe their metaphors. Jesus was doing this sort of reframing each time he told people, "You have heard it said, but I say . . ."

Photographer/essayist Robert Adams defines art as "an attempt, by fond attention to the world, to find redeeming metaphor in it."[2] Christians already have all the requisite redeeming metaphors. What Briggs and Hyatt provide in this book are wise words on how we can develop a "fond attention to the world" so that we can put those redeeming metaphors to work through mantras.

If everything can be said better with metaphor than without, then every metaphor can be said better as a mantra. And this is why you need this book as a resource and reminder. A meme is a metaphor with an attitude and a drive. It wants to reproduce itself, mutating as it moves through the culture. But for a metaphor to become a meme it needs to first be a mantra. A mantra turns a metaphor into a cognitive grappling hook—a sound bite that bites.

I have a secret mission in life: to raise up a mafia of the metaphor. The godfather (small "g") of the metaphor mafia is C. S. Lewis, who didn't start with words for the tales of Narnia. He started with images, and then trusted the words to come. But the real Godfather (capital "G") of the metaphor mafia is Jesus. He trained his disciples to be a mafia of the metaphor with a mission: infiltrate to filtrate the water and blood of the body with healing metaphors.

Thanks to Bob Hyatt and J.R. Briggs, we now have a manual of camo clothing and gear to take with us on that mission.

INTRODUCTION

The Power of Mantras

mantra [mahn-*truh*]
noun

1. A word, formula, incantation or prayer chanted or sung.
2. An often-repeated word, formula or phrase, often a truism.

For it is good to keep these sayings in your heart
and always ready on your lips.

PROVERBS 22:18 (NLT)

In July 2011, Guy Kawasaki presented a brief talk at Stanford University's Entrepreneurship Corner titled "Don't Write a Mission Statement, Write a Mantra."[1] Kawasaki shared that while each organization seeks to develop a clear and compelling mission statement, it would be more effective to develop a mantra—a short phrase that captures the essence of your organization while also capturing the attention of others. Why? Because nobody remembers verbose mission statements full of buzzwords that sound significant but actually say little of substance.

Mission, no doubt, is crucial; knowing who you are and what you're after is vital to any group of people. But mission statements can be long, clunky and difficult to remember (and even difficult to comprehend). Mantras, however—these pithy, catchy, significant and easily remembered phrases—can cast vision and bring clarity in smaller, bite-sized portions.

Local churches are distinct from secular organizations in motivation, mission, philosophy and expression. But as church leaders we should take note of what Kawasaki is saying. Because mantras deliver clear communication in punchy, wise, truthful and memorable ways, they can serve a purpose in rallying God's people around God's mission in a particular context. *Mission statements are good, but mantras are better.*

WHAT ARE MANTRAS?

Colin Powell once said, "Leaders have simple phrases constantly repeated." For something to be simple it must be reproducible. And for something to be reproducible it must be simple. Therefore, for culture to stick it must be simple, easy to remember and easily transferable. Mantras can help leaders in this way.

Specifically, a mantra contains four elements: (1) it is wise and truthful, (2) the message is clear, (3) it is compelling and (4) it is memorable—oftentimes the shorter the mantra, the more memorable it can be. Mantras are mottos you can hang your hat on. They are phrases that can be constantly repeated; they are simple, but not simplistic. Mantras are not rules or policies, formulas or equations. They are the paint we use on the canvas of our contexts to create a picture of what we value.

Inventor, printer and American statesman Ben Franklin is known for his wise mantras. "Well done is better than well said." "Early to bed and early to rise makes a man healthy, wealthy and wise." "Remember that time is money." "No pain, no gain." "Haste makes waste." Many of his mantras have shaped the American imagination—even today. Think of Yoda and his use of mantras throughout the *Star Wars* films. Undoubtedly his most famous line was "Do or do not. There is no try."

Discerning how to eat healthily has become quite complicated. Several years ago, my wife and I wanted to eat healthily but were left confused by what healthy eating actually meant. Different health studies seemed to contradict previous studies, and reading food labels led to further confusion. Food-health advocate and writer Michael Pollan wanted to help the millions of confused Americans like my wife and me by cutting through the complexity. As a result he wrote the book *Food Rules: An Eater's Manual*, and in it he aimed for simplicity and clarity:

> I realized that the answer to the supposedly incredibly complicated question of what we should eat wasn't so complicated after all, and in fact could be boiled down to just seven words: *Eat food. Not too much. Mostly plants.* This was the bottom line, and it was satisfying to have found it, a piece of hard ground deep down at the bottom of the swamp of nutrition science: seven words of plain English, no biochemistry degree required.[2]

In his book, Pollan included sixty-four brief, compelling and memorable food fundamentals centered on those three principles: *Eat food. Not too much. Mostly plants.* Here are some of my favorites:

> If it came from a plant, eat it. If it was made in a plant, don't.
>
> It's not food if it arrived through the window of your car.
>
> Eat when you're hungry, not when you're bored.
>
> Don't get your fuel from the same place your car does.[3]

After reading Pollan's short book, my wife and I found that his ways to choose healthy eating habits made sense. Because they were concise, truthful and memorable, many of the food rules would come to my mind just as I was tempted to go back for seconds, to put a pint of ice cream in my cart at the grocery store, or to pull into the drive-through lane at Wendy's. Though he never uses the term in the book, Pollan, in essence, wrote a book of food mantras.

Healthy nations and healthy eating are all well and good, but this book is about healthy churches. As ministry leaders who have been given a sacred calling, we need simplicity in an age of seemingly ever-increasing complexity. We seek and submit to the Holy Spirit's guidance in our lives. We study and apply scriptural truths. But we also need ministry wisdom based on lived-out experience—and it needs to be unmistakably clear. Ministry mantras are not naïve and mindless oversimplification; they are guiding principles to help navigate the complex world of ministry with confidence, clarity and wisdom.

We see mantras throughout the Scriptures. The Psalms and Proverbs are full of wise, life-giving and memorable sayings that offer sound instruction.

Jesus had his own mantras ("Be as shrewd as snakes and as innocent as doves" [Matthew 10:16]; "It is not the healthy who need a doctor, but the sick" [Matthew 9:12]; "You will know the truth, and the truth will set you free" [John 8:32]), as did Paul ("Follow my example, as I follow the example of Christ" [1 Corinthians 11:1]; "I can do all things through Christ who strengthens me" [Philippians 4:13 NKJV]; "Do not be anxious about anything" [Philippians 4:6]). And one of the earliest mantras in the Christian church is *kyrie eleison*, "Lord, have mercy," oft repeated by our Eastern Orthodox brothers and sisters. The hearts and minds of millions of Christians have been shaped by these mantras.

WHY MANTRAS?

For years I've asked myself, *What phrases can we use—or continue to use—with frequency and purpose in order to instill, remind and embed what we value in the culture of our church?* I'll brainstorm phrases and write them down in my notebook. I'll pray over them. I'll ask the Lord to reveal something to our elders that we can latch on to in describing what a life with God looks like. But sometimes mantras show up unexpectedly. Occasionally, someone in our church family will say something in a leaders' meeting or over coffee or in an email that rings true with who we are in a memorable way. "Wow. I like that," I tell them. "That really resonates with who we are as a church. We're going to repeat that in various settings."

Words are one of the most important tools available to leaders. Marshall Goldsmith wrote, "If there's one thing we've learned in this noisy media age, it's that simple, un-nuanced messages break through the clutter and hit home with high impact."[4] As the mantra goes, *language creates culture.* Therefore, we want to be able to use phrases that speak to what we value most. As pastors, our prayer is that what we value most is what Jesus values most. Mantras provide a shared vocabulary for localized Jesus communities. That shared vocabulary serves as a cohesive glue that reinforces cultural identity and encourages communal rhythms.

I like to ask leaders in our church, "How would you describe our church in a few sentences or phrases?" I want to see if some of our mantras are sticking. To be clear, mantras are quite different from pithy quotes posted on your church marquee. And mantras are different from what some churches use to describe their vision, posting a few catchy words such as: "Come. See. Grow. Go," or "Celebrate. Serve. Send," on literature in the lobby or a banner in the sanctuary. Those might be helpful, but this is not what I mean when I speak of mantras.

When I share the vision of our church using a few of our church's mantras with leaders or longtime church members, they sometimes say, "We know, we know. We've heard you say that a dozen times before." It reveals that these mantras are taking root. I want our leaders, should someone stop and ask them what our church is all about, to be able to share these mantras.

Mantras are important enough to the culture of our churches that they oftentimes guide our decision-making processes. Sometimes one of our leaders will ask, "How might this decision fit into our mantra that says . . . ?" Mantras act as a compass, reorienting us when we're uncertain where to go next.

WHY ARE MANTRAS IMPORTANT?

Mantras can be helpful, but they are only effective when they are actually lived out. God desires for kingdom agents not just to talk a good game, but to act upon it in obedience.

Joel Limbauan, a key volunteer at our church, graduated from film school and runs his own film production company. Our leaders asked Joel to create a short film that we could show others to give people a glimpse of who we are as a church. With little involvement or direction from the elders or staff, Joel wrote the script. Here's what ended up in the video:

> We are The Renew Community. A family where no perfect people are allowed,[5] a place for the hurting and the hungry.
>
> We are a group of people learning to pay attention to God and to respond appropriately.[6] We aim to know Jesus and to become like him.
>
> We are missionaries cleverly disguised as good neighbors.
>
> We are an ally and an advocate for our community asking, "How can we help?" and "How can we serve?"
>
> We meet in gyms and in homes, in backyards and on front porches. We are led by the Holy Spirit, and we submit our structure to his.[7]

We want to be part of God's mission, and we want to be known more for our sending capacity than our seating capacity.[8]

Quite simply, we at Renew just want to live up to our name.

We believe that we have been renewed by God.

We are constantly in the process of being renewed.

And we are attempting to join with God in the renewal of all things.

What encouraged the elders and pastors most was that Joel included in the video several mantras that we use regularly in our church family (nine to be exact). Because we use mantras frequently and purposefully in a variety of contexts, Joel has picked them up along the way, and they have become a part of his communicative instincts in describing who we are and what we value.

This is the power of mantras within a local church.

THE LIMITS OF PROVERBIAL WISDOM

Mantras and proverbs describe wisdom for *most* but not all situations. They speak to a general truth that often has exceptions and requires discernment in its application. Even the book of Proverbs shows the limits of proverbial wisdom and the discernment needed when applying it to situations. These two proverbs are found back to back in the same chapter: "Don't answer the foolish arguments of fools, or you will become as foolish as they are. Be sure to answer the foolish arguments of fools, or they will become wise in their own estimation" (Proverbs 26:4-5 NLT). The writer of Proverbs isn't contradicting himself here, but rather pointing to the nature of axiomatic wisdom and the need to discern when and where to apply it. See these mantras not as laws describing how things ought always to be done, but as general wisdom for most (but not all) ministry situations.

Albert Einstein said, "Simplify as much as possible, but no more." It's a wise leader who can discern limits as she or he applies these mantras. They are simple, but we need wisdom lest we become simplistic or formulaic in their application.

WHY WE WROTE THE BOOK

While this book addresses leadership, the primary emphasis is ministry. Certainly, ministry entails leadership, but followership to Christ is of greater importance. What we're after is developing cultures where Jesus is central, the kingdom is sought after, discipleship is key, fulfilling the Great Commission is the focus and loving our neighbors is the goal. But the bucket of vision in our church (as in every church) has tiny pinholes in it. It leaks and needs frequent refilling. Mantras are a way to help refill the bucket with clarity and memory. If language creates culture, then the right kind of mantras used at the appropriate time, place and frequency can help to cultivate a mission-aligned ethos within a local Jesus community. Our friend Bryan Long developed his own mantra on this topic: "Values are nonnegotiable and leader-protected, but rhythms are negotiable and community-discerned." Kingdom leaders are the primary cultivators and protectors of the values embodied in a local church, but how those are expressed is worked out with the people within the local church.

The mantras in this book are not some theoretical list of catchy phrases we came up with on a whiteboard during a brainstorming session. Each one is used frequently in a variety of settings—sermons, leadership community meetings, discipleship, breakfast meetings, late-night conversations over coffee and conversations with strangers. They are deeply embedded into the vernacular of our churches.

While we've latched on to these mantras, we don't expect or desire you to use all of these in your particular context. In fact, doing so may be unhelpful. We are convinced that a "speak-by-number" approach to ministry is lifeless and impersonal. We want to encourage you to use discernment. Use some of these mantras in your own contexts, tweak others and disregard others still. Just don't try to strap on King Saul's armor. Our hope is to get Spirit-inspired juices flowing to help you create mantras that work for your context, unique to the plot of ground God has entrusted to you. A practical suggestion while you read: circle or highlight key phrases, metaphors or concepts that jump out at you—or jot down new words or phrases in the margins.

Ministry mantras are not bumper-sticker theology. They are not for ministry branding, marketing or publicity purposes. They are intended to provide wisdom and clarity in order to ignite kingdom imagination and engagement. They are the proverbial seeds of kingdom values planted in local communities of faith.

Instead of being organized into ten or twelve lengthy chapters, as you may find in a typical book, this book is purposefully different, composed of almost eighty short chapters of one to three pages of explanation. All of the mantras used are original to us and our churches, unless otherwise noted. As we mentioned previously, we have adopted some mantras from other leaders and pastors. This is in part what we hope that you will do as well. We've attempted to give credit where credit is due. Any unaccredited reference is purely accidental.

Part One

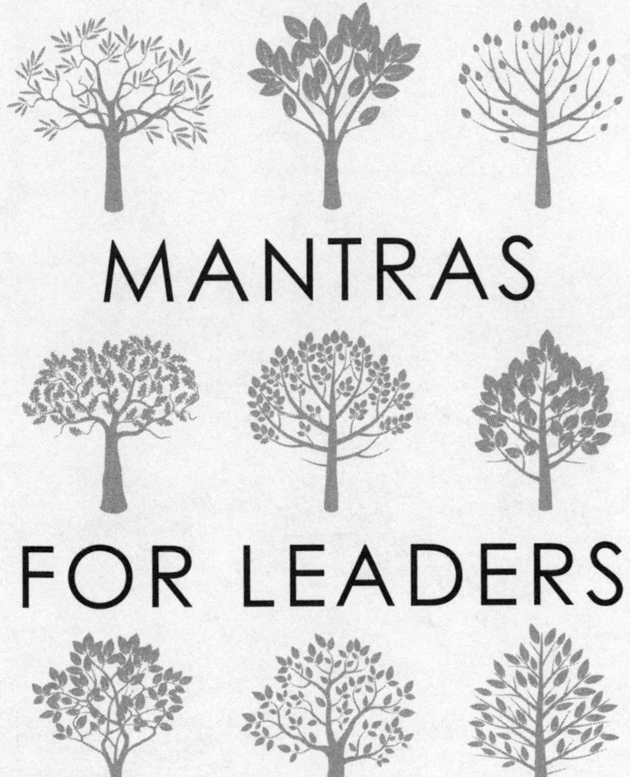

MANTRAS FOR LEADERS

SECTION ONE

Leadership

A Leader Is a Culture Cultivator

J.R.

Leaders are culture cultivators, gardeners who possess a calling to cultivate faithfully a plot of ground entrusted to their care. If leaders are culture cultivators, then the question needs to be asked: What, exactly, is culture?

Culture is the set of accepted rhythms, values, practices and unwritten laws of a particular group or subgroup. Culture is often revealed in the values we hold dear, the language we use regularly, the stories we tell most often (and how we tell them) and the rhythms we participate in.

Therefore, as people called to lead God's people, we should be asking a series of questions such as the following:

- What do we celebrate, and why these particular things?
- What do we hold most dear?
- What is it that we mourn?
- What language do we use to describe the nature of reality?
- What "stories of legend" do we tell most frequently—and why these?
- What are the rhythms of our lives? And what does that say about who we are and what we care about?

When you think about your culture—a set of accepted rhythms, practices, values and language in your particular Jesus community—consider what it says about who your community is, how you see the world and, ultimately, how you view and interact with God.

One of Peter Drucker's most popular mantras is "Culture eats strategy for breakfast." Leaders are called to care about the culture entrusted to them and to work hard to cultivate a culture that embodies what it should care about most.

Jesus created culture by announcing the new reality with his arrival. He used imaginative language, he told stories of celebration, and he honored people's stories when they embraced a culture of the kingdom of God. The language he employed ("The kingdom of God is like . . ."), the symbols he used (sheep, a party, bread, water, a servant's towel, the cross, etc.), and the rhythms he participated in (prayer, worship, rest, justice, service, generosity, healing, caring for those others had ignored or scorned, etc.) all created a new culture. When I travel and people ask me what I do, I usually tell them I am a culture cultivator. Inquisitive people follow up and ask me to explain specifically what I do. I tell them I help a local church care most about the things that Jesus cares most about.

As spiritual leaders, it is much more important to cultivate a kingdom culture than it is to build quality programs. Programs aren't inherently wrong, but they are often overemphasized. Ultimately, our call isn't to develop stellar programs; it's to see that the values of the kingdom run through the collective bloodstream of our churches. Commit to cultivating a healthy kingdom-centered ethos—*then* allow programs, events and initiatives to flow out of that culture.

Fruitful leaders are the ones who regularly ask, "What kind of culture are we seeking to cultivate here—and does it align with the values of the kingdom Jesus came to bring to earth?" Create a culture that seeks to care most about the things that Jesus cares most about.

It's About Form, Not Formula—Intention, Not Equation

J.R.

One of the most crucial elements of leading a church is finding the appropriate balance between having too little structure and creating too much. Pastors with overstructured churches allow little to no room for change, should God want to interrupt their plans. When we trust in our methods more than our Messiah, we miss the point of being the church Jesus desires.

Conversely, several church leaders—many of them younger—believe structure is inherently bad and should be avoided at all costs in the church. They speak of an "organic" approach to church. Without knowing it, they reveal their assumptions that *organic* is synonymous with *unstructured.* Organic gardens are not places where gardeners haphazardly scatter seeds in whatever direction they desire. No, structure is present in organic gardens; the carrots are here, the corn there and the tomatoes over there to the right. In fact, organic gardens oftentimes have *more* structure than non-organic gardens. The word *organic* doesn't mean unstructured; it means all natural, without any artificial enhancement. If you want to have an "organic" church, structure is still necessary.

Many of Paul's letters to the house churches scattered around Asia Minor included instruction and correction about their structures. Paul provides guidance to their structure, but he doesn't provide every little detail, allowing them to work it out in their particular context. It's important to remember: structure isn't detrimental to mission, but overstructure can be.

A few churches we know have a simple three-pronged approach to their structure: lightweight, low maintenance, high accountability. Their approach is thoughtful and purposeful, yet flexible and interruptible. Conversely, missionless churches believe that their sole mission is to perpetuate what has always been done. Their mission is to follow the manual, while missing the promptings of the Spirit. This is not to say that church history or traditions are unimportant. They have value and are important for us to understand our heritage. While tradition and history can be respected, they should never be worshiped. The purpose of our churches was never intended to perpetuate the "good old days." The Spirit is never formulaic, but that doesn't mean that churches shouldn't be purposeful and intentional in developing vision, rhythms and structure.

Healthy church structures can be dynamic and flexible, not static and rigid. Paul's instructions about structure to the church in Corinth were quite different from his instructions to the church in Colossae, Philippi and Ephesus, while the focus of the mission was the same. We've worshiped and served in house churches, megachurches and church plants in denominational and nondenominational structures. We've seen local Jesus communities meet in beautiful church buildings, gyms, pubs, parks, bars, storefronts, restaurants and living rooms. At their best, church structures grow and develop over time. No particular church structure should be universalized and made absolute as a mandatory structure for all local churches.

The key element in developing our church structures is listening to the Spirit while using wisdom and discernment to know just how much structure we can provide that would allow us to be nimble and flexible, yet focused and sustainable, to help God's people join God's mission through God's Spirit—wherever he desires us to be and whatever he desires us to do.

Many times when we gather before one of our Sunday gatherings with our worship team, tech team and other leaders, someone will pray: "God, interrupt our plans if you need to! We give you permission. We've done our part to plan and pray and prepare, but if you have other more important things for us this morning, do that instead."

Have form, but don't make it formulaic. Be intentional with your church structures—just don't turn them into an impersonal equation.

Leadership Is Purposefully Choosing Whom You Will Disappoint

J.R.

Leadership is incredibly difficult when we ignore tough conversations and turn away from crucial conversations. At times, having these conversations can be an excruciating task, especially for people pleasers.

Leaders know the sting of letting people down. Leaders also know that their role requires making decisions that aren't always liked or well received. But sometimes we as leaders feel more than a sting. Sometimes there are scars—and even gaping wounds—inflicted by close friends, key volunteers, leaders, former friends, congregants and critics (sometimes even our own family members) who have expressed their disappointment and frustration in no uncertain terms.

Abraham Lincoln has been credited with (though not proven) saying, "You can fool all of the people some of the time, and some of the people all of the time, but you cannot fool all the people all the time." It's also fair to say, "You can please all of the people some of the time, and some of the people all of the time, but you cannot please all of the people all of the time." Sometimes we can forget that there is a significant difference between leadership and appeasement.

As a leader, Jesus was willing to disappoint everyone except his Father. Let that sink in for a moment. Jesus disappointed his disciples, the religious leaders, the crowds and his closest friends—

even his own mother. But he was never willing to disappoint his heavenly Father. Everything he did was rooted in the motivation to do only what he saw his Father doing (see John 5).

Additionally, Jesus purposefully chose to disappoint certain groups of people more than others. In fact, *Jesus seemed to go out of his way to disappoint, challenge, agitate—even infuriate—the religious leaders of the day.* Pharisees, Sadducees, and the scribes and teachers of the law were constantly at odds with him. Jesus seemed to expend a great amount of energy to challenge them. He told stories where the plot unmistakably would reveal that they were not the heroes, but the villains. When they would try to trap him, he would find a way to catch them in their own trap. He healed on the Sabbath just to tick them off. Couldn't he have waited twenty-four hours to heal a shriveled hand? He even disappointed his own disciples. Why? Because what they wanted was quite different from Jesus' mission on earth.

And yet did you notice Jesus hardly disappointed those on the margins—the poor, the forgotten, the hurt, the broken and the left out? Richard Rohr reminds us that Jesus is never upset with sinners; he's only upset with people who think they are not sinners! Jesus lived up to his own mantra: it's not the healthy who need a doctor, but the sick. He was known as a *friend of sinners.* Let that sink in.

In the beginning stages of our church, we knew that we'd attract all sorts of new people to our church, simply out of curiosity about something new. In our elder meetings we had to ask, "Who are the people we are willing to disappoint?" Initially, it felt strange—even wrong—to ask. But we knew that our church wasn't going to please everyone. Entitled people cause damage to Jesus' mission. Contrary to popular opinion, nobody owes us anything. Not even God. *Healthy churches work purposefully to disappoint religiously entitled people.*

We looked carefully at the types of people Jesus chose to disappoint. We found that he disappointed those who wanted religion—even Christian religion—on *their* terms. He disappointed those who thought they had it all together, which kept them from hanging out with and loving those who were convinced they did not. So we made a difficult but necessary decision that we must be willing to disappoint religiously entitled people. Oftentimes it's not the effects of godlessness that destroy the souls of Christians, but rather the effects of religiosity. In our first few years, we noticed that the more people felt religiously entitled, the quicker they left our church. And deep down, we were okay with that. Still other times we were deeply grateful.

As a leader—and as a church—who are you willing to disappoint?

It's More Important to Be a Servant Who Leads Than a Leader Who Serves

J.R.

The term *servant leadership* might win the award for the most overused ministry buzzword of the past fifteen years. It's not limited to ministry discussions and pastors' conferences anymore; servant leadership language is used frequently in business, politics, education, medicine and technology. So, what is servant leadership *really?*

As a wet-behind-the-ears pastor in my first year of full-time vocational ministry, my mentor Tom asked me a question over lunch that still remains with me: "Which is more important: to be a leader who serves, or a servant who leads?" He let me wrestle with that question for a few minutes before he answered. Tom shared that servanthood is our foundational identity as followers of Christ, while leadership is *what we do out of that identity*. If leadership is our identity and servanthood is what we do as leaders, we have our priorities mixed up. Tom pressed in further. If you're a leader who serves, and all of a sudden that leadership position is taken away from you for whatever reason, you'll be rocked to your core because your identity has been taken away from you. But if you are a servant who leads, and your leadership role is taken away from you, you can still be a servant even though your leadership is expressed differently now as one who files papers or answers phones, or cleans toilets or takes out the trash.

I've met many "servant leaders" who tell me that they are called to lead. But when those leadership roles require them to roll up their sleeves and get messy in thankless behind-the-scenes roles, they begin to make excuses, complain or start devising an exit plan. They are leaders in name only. As Mike Pilavachi said so profoundly, "If serving is below you, then leadership is above you."

Jesus, God in the flesh, washing his disciples' feet continues to inspire, clarify, challenge and confront our view of leadership (see John 13). An act only to be done by the lowest of servants in a first-century home stopped Peter in his tracks. So scandalous was the act that he told Jesus he wouldn't allow it. Yet Jesus insisted. What is astounding is that Jesus washed the feet of both Judas and Peter. One of the Twelve would eventually betray him willingly—another would end up denying him serially. *And yet Jesus, knowing all of this, washed their feet anyway.* Radical love is the willingness to wash peoples' feet, even though you know they will end up betraying and denying you. Our friend A. J. Swoboda once wrote, "Name one other god who washes feet." Only a humble servant who leads would do something that radical.

Paul described this servant-who-leads posture of Jesus in Philippians 2—as the one who would cast off all temptation to grasp at power in order to serve humanity. The world longs to see more John 13 and Philippians 2 leaders, who gain influence not by wielding power or demanding authority, but through a willingness to serve at all costs. Being a servant leader is a noble calling—as long as it's rooted in the identity of a servant.

Structure Must Always Submit to Spirit

J.R.

How would we know when our church structures have become an idol?

When we were in the early formation stages of planting our church, I stumbled upon this mantra from pastor, author and kingdom entrepreneur Erwin McManus.[1] We believed it would be one of the most important values we could adopt in the life of our church. In fact, it became the first official mantra of our church. We've used this phrase countless times.

Tragically, we've interacted with churches that espouse the opposite value: Spirit must always submit to structure. They would never openly admit it, but the way they operate and the values they embrace—even the language they use—sends a clear and unmistakable message. On the other hand, when we look at the book of Acts, we see the early church excitedly seeking and following the direction of the Holy Spirit. With no church history, Book of Order, denominational polity or church hierarchy, all they had to rely upon was faith in the Spirit's work and the memory of the words of their Lord and teacher, Jesus.

The new wine and new wineskin concept Jesus taught is found in all three of the Synoptic Gospels. As wine ferments, it emits gases; thus, a nimble, flexible vessel was needed to store wine in order to adapt to the changing of the gases. Wineskins were made of fresh and pliable animal skins. They had to be. As the fermenting wine released gases, the wineskins would expand and contract.

Over time and with much use, the animal skins would lose their elasticity and become brittle, often cracking and becoming useless. Our vessels (structures) should be nimble to hold the wine (the Spirit's work). We must never forget that the purpose of the wineskin is to hold the wine. *The wineskin serves the needs of the wine, not the other way around.*

In our book *Eldership and the Mission of God*, we wrote about the Costco milk container.[2] If you've bought milk at Costco before, you know the shape of their milk containers is quite different from the look and shape of traditional milk containers. It was a radical redesign: a taller, square-like shape with a larger spout. Costco desired an easily stackable product, which would make a more efficient shipping process, and thus, the milk would arrive at stores faster and therefore fresher. Increased efficiency also lowered costs for customers.

All this sounds well and good—until you begin to use the newly designed milk container. Each time I poured, the milk hugged the edge of the container all the way to the bottom and spilled all over the kitchen counter. It was a mess. When the container was empty a few days later, we guessed that more milk ended up on our kitchen counter and table than in our glasses and breakfast bowls. Theologically speaking, Costco milk containers are a result of the fall. It was our first—and last—Costco milk purchase. Innovative, cutting-edge, more efficient, fresher and cost-effective? Sure. But that's not the point of a milk container. The simple purpose of the container should be to pour milk effectively into a bowl or a glass. All of the innovative changes didn't matter. *The company forgot that the purpose of the container is to serve the milk, not the other way around.*

We often forget this with our churches. We spend a lot of time and energy on our containers, making them innovative, cutting-edge, aesthetically pleasing and more efficient. Yet we forget that the purpose of the wineskin is to hold the wine appropriately and pour it out. *It's about the wine, not the wineskin!*

Our call as church leaders is to create structures that allow us to keep the milk the priority. We have an important part to play in stewarding the work of God—and then pouring it out into a world in need, by the power of the Spirit.[3] Yes, this involves risk and uncertainty. At times, it can make leading a church more difficult and less comfortable, but if we truly believe the milk is of great value, then our containers should serve the milk, not the other way around.

When we create pliable structures, it allows God's Spirit to move and for us to follow the Spirit faithfully and effectively as we discern the Spirit's leading. Don't allow the *we've never done it that way before* mindset to dictate your decision-making processes in your church.

Structures are important, but not as important as what the Spirit wants to do in, among and through you. Make the milk—not the container—the priority in your church.

SECTION TWO

Vision

Bet the Farm on Discipleship

J.R.

Many churches believe discipleship is important, but few bet the farm on it.

Alan Hirsch described discipleship as the "irreplaceable and lifelong task of becoming like Jesus by embodying His message."[1] Regardless of size, age, denomination or tradition, every church is charged to make disciples—this is the Great Commission. But many churches fall on either end of a spectrum: the Great Commotion, creating unending spiritual programs for people with the belief it will automatically lead to discipleship, or the Great Omission, doing nothing related to discipleship.

Spiritual activity does not lead to discipleship and frenetic activity does not equate to spiritual health, no matter how "spiritual" it may seem. At the same time, nobody drifts into a committed, growing relationship with Christ. Nobody wakes up one day and says, "I'm not sure how it happened, but without really knowing it, I am a lot like Jesus in every area of my life." It takes a purposeful pursuit in the lives of individuals and entire communities of Jesus. It also takes an ongoing and purposeful pursuit by the leaders of a local church. Leaders: *if you do only one thing in your church, make disciples—and if you don't know how, learn how.*

The closer we get to Jesus, the more he requires of us—and frees us. Discipleship isn't merely a class or an eight-week program you offer, where at the completion of the course people are automatically like Jesus. It's not a series of rules and regulations, nor is it a moral checklist of dos and don'ts.

Dallas Willard said that every church must ask two crucial questions: What is our process of discipleship? Does it work? Every few months the leaders of key areas of our church gather for an evening to plan out the basic schedule of the year. We look at our gatherings, teaching series, kids' ministry, men's and women's retreats, baptisms, youth retreats and other events. Each leader is called upon to answer clearly and compellingly how each of these particular events he or she oversees will assist people in their growth as disciples of Christ. We are not committed to filling up people's calendars with religious activities; instead we are committed to leading people to become fully devoted, committed and passionate followers of Christ. If our leaders cannot connect each specific event or initiative to discipleship, we cut it. We want to make sure that discipleship is not a mere hood ornament on the rhythms of our church, but the central goal around which everything orbits.

But it's deeper than just scheduling meetings. What we present as the gospel will ultimately determine what we present as discipleship. If the gospel is simply "say a prayer and you're all set"—fire-insurance policy—then there is no need for discipleship. But if the gospel is inviting people into the Way of Jesus to live into the values of the kingdom of God, then discipleship is absolutely essential to right living.

Neil Cole wrote, "Ultimately each church will be evaluated by only one thing: its disciples. Your church is only as good as its disciples. It does not matter how good your praise, preaching, programs or property are: If your disciples are passive, needy, consumerist, and not moving in the direction of radical obedience, your church is not good."[2] Are you willing to go that far in how you evaluate the effectiveness of your own church? If so, ask yourself: Do our schedules, church calendars, facilities and budgets clearly reflect that our church's main priority is to make disciples, or do they reveal a desire merely to keep our congregation busy?

Many spiritual activities—good as they may seem—can actually distract and detract us from what we are called to pursue: making disciples (see Matthew 28:18-20). There are a lot of busy people in churches, but we're not after making people tired or busy. *We're after making disciples of Jesus.* And those disciples should look like sheep from up front and like shepherds from behind. Refuse to construct religious hamster wheels for people. This may even mean calling our people to do *less,* not more, in order to encourage their growth and formation as disciples of Jesus.

As other leaders have said, don't build the church. That's Jesus' job. We're called to make disciples. Be about the business of the Father, not the busyness of the church. If your church fails to make disciples, your church fails.

Every Church Is Born Pregnant

J.R.

It's a basic principle of biology: *healthy things reproduce.* Whether tomato plants or rabbits or humans, healthy organisms reproduce. The same is true for churches. It may involve planting churches out of your church, or it may involve starting new small groups or discipling new believers or equipping and unleashing people in your congregation to start "kingdom experiments" in the neighborhood. Healthy churches reproduce disciples.

Several years ago, after I took some extended time away in silence and solitude, the Lord revealed to me something profound and deeply personal. I pulled out a yellow legal pad and scribbled down the thought:

The prompting was that now was the time to move from leadership by addition to leadership by multiplication. The ministry-by-addition approach, which asked, "How many people were in church Sunday morning?" needed to be replaced by a ministry-by-multiplication posture, which asked, "How are we equipping and unleashing disciples of Jesus into the world in order to represent Christ?" Paul tells the church in Ephesus that God gives people different gifts in order to "equip his people for works of service, so that the body of Christ may be built up until we all reach unity in the faith and in the knowledge of the Son of God and become mature, attaining to the whole measure of the fullness of Christ" (Ephesians 4:12-13). He later writes that we should excel in the spiritual gifts that build up the church (see 1 Corinthians 14:12). Healthy churches think, structure and embody a multiplicative mindset.

Our church has an unusual structure. We don't meet as an entire church every weekend. We meet altogether in what we call gatherings every other week, while on alternate weeks we meet in smaller, geographically based groupings of people in what we call house churches. Admittedly, our structure is nontraditional and, at times, can feel a bit clunky. But as we seek to structure for multiplication and not just addition, we believe that in our context in the northern reaches of the greater Philadelphia area, this sets us up for the best opportunity to equip the people entrusted to us to become disciples for Christ in a multiplicative manner.

Structuring for multiplication sounds great, but it requires great sacrifice. Entrusting half of our formal teaching and leadership responsibilities every month to the leaders of our house churches can be a risk. If we don't disciple, train, equip and unleash our leaders to use their gifts, our structure would fall apart, quite literally, in two weeks. In the parable of the seed and the sower, just a fraction of the seed falls on healthy soil, but that seed will reap a harvest thirty-, sixty-, even a hundredfold. Healthy soil has a multiplicative effect on organisms.

I have the privilege of serving alongside Doug Moister, another pastor in our church community. Convinced that our church is born pregnant, Doug and I talk regularly about the School Bus Principle. We ask: "If we were both walking across a busy street, and a school bus struck and killed us instantly, what would happen to our church?" (Morbid as it may sound, it is a significant question worth pondering in every church context). If our church would be incompetent and completely unprepared if we were no longer around, then we have failed to lead our church faithfully. If, however, we work now to equip and prepare our church in the unlikely (and undesired!) circumstance of our absence, we may succeed. We hope our church family would miss us (at least for a few weeks). But we also hope that they would know deep down to their core that they are loved, equipped and empowered and that they have been unleashed to lead, serve and love out of their giftedness.

In their book *Growing Spiritual Redwoods*, Bill Easum and Tom Bandy write that spiritual leaders are like midwives.[1] For years I viewed my leadership as if I was a mother, giving birth to my own ideas and visions. But Easum and Bandy helped me realize that kingdom leaders help *others* give birth to their God-given dreams. As leaders we aren't mothers; we are midwives. But this means that if we truly want to equip others, we have to get out of the center of the story. Few people have a picture of their midwife in their baby book. The focus is on the mother and child. And yet the role of a midwife is significant in the birthing process. Every church is born pregnant; therefore, help the mothers in your church birth kingdom babies.

God Uses Crazy People to See the Kingdom Expanded

J.R.

Planting a church can strip you bare and draw out every possible insecurity.

"Are we going to make it financially?"

"Will God be faithful and help us through this?"

"Will anyone want to join with us in our efforts?"

But the most common question—the one that went through my mind more than once each week for the first few years—was "Have I lost my mind? Am I just crazy?" In that lonely and unsettling season of ministry, I longed for a wise, experienced church planter to pull me aside and assure me. "No, J.R., you're fine. You're doing just what you should be doing." But that never happened.

Each year I, along with several of my ministry friends, including Bob, attend the Ecclesia Network National Gathering.[1] In the first few years of attending, I prayed that God would surround me with people who would assure me with what I thought I needed to hear—"No, J.R., you are not crazy." Yet in that first year God answered my prayer—but in a way I hadn't envisioned. As I sat in a room with other faith-filled and passionate church planters, the Lord impressed upon me a word I have never forgotten: *Yes, J.R., you* are *crazy. But I use crazy people to impact the kingdom of God through church planting. You are crazy—but you are not alone. I use crazy people like you for my purposes.*

It was not what I had originally wanted to hear, but it was—and still is—exactly what I need to hear. It was the affirmation I needed.

When we read the book of Acts, we can't help but be captured by the radical nature of the early disciples. With no formal theological training, no denominational support, no church history, and little knowledge and direction about structure, protocol or experience, they boldly and faithfully followed God's Spirit. They were ordinary people crazy enough to take God at his word. The Spirit's presence was enough for this crazy group of people to be willing to follow Christ wherever and whenever he went.

Imagine if radical was the norm. What if we embraced—and even encouraged—the craziness in our faith in Christ? Certainly, we need equal measures of wisdom and courage. But too often we speak of "wisdom" as merely an excuse for refusing to jump in and take faith-fueled risks that honor God's heart. We play it safe, hedge our bets and drift toward comfort and ease—and then wonder why we aren't seeing the kind of impact we expect in our churches. Our God is not safe, and our Christ is not predictable; shall we follow them in that way?

Equilibrium is the precursor to death.[2] The world doesn't need more sensible and respectable Christians who do what we've always done. We need more crazy Christians—in all the best ways possible. As leaders our calling is to make the radical commitment to Jesus and his kingdom the norm. Refuse to be comfortable with leading a church that strives to be comfortable. And don't ever forget that you're crazy—and that's a good thing.

Don't Try to Make Church Relevant to the Crowds; Make the Gospel Relatable to the Context

J.R.

We cringe when we hear pastors tell us they want their churches to be relevant. Relevancy is overrated.

We don't think Jesus cared one bit about churches being "relevant" by keeping up with the times and trying to fit into the culture. What he cared about was making the kingdom of God—God's ultimate rule and reign—accessible, compelling, available and clear to the world he loves. Our pursuit shouldn't be creating a relevant church, but making the gospel relatable to our context.

Paul's missionary posture at Mars Hill has significant implications for our time (see Acts 17:16-34). One thing is for sure: Paul wasn't striving to be cool, hip, relevant or cutting-edge in the Athenian culture. As he waits for Silas and Timothy to join him, he is greatly distressed by the amount of idols he sees (see Acts 17:16). Many people believe that in Athens there were more gods than men. Paul tries to help people see how the life, death and resurrection of Jesus relate specifically to their lives—and why that matters.

Despite his distress, he doesn't first stand up and condemn them of their idolatry. He walks around the area and looks carefully and critically at their culture, noticing their gods and idols. He reasons with them in the synagogues and with the Greeks in the marketplace (see Acts 17:17), what sociologists would call "third places."[1]

He listens to what they care about and how their culture works (see Acts 17:18-21). When he speaks with them, he quotes two of their revered thinkers, Cretan philosopher Epimenides and Cilician Stoic philosopher Aratus (see Acts 17:28). And after studying, noticing and learning, he acknowledges the altar in their community—titled "To an Unknown God." He uses that cultural artifact to build a bridge of connection and to communicate that this unknown god is actually someone who Paul knows and who is capable of being known by the Athenians as well. It's then—and only then—that he begins to proclaim the good news of Jesus. He uses what he sees in their context—their culture, their poets, their worldview—in order to relate the gospel message to their lives.

To have a posture that longs to make the gospel relatable to our context means being humble and patient and thinking missiologically like Paul at Mars Hill. To possess this posture of humility means we have to learn to explore and exegete our communities with the same passion as we exegete the Scriptures. It means becoming experts of our zip codes by learning, listening, walking around, discussing and interacting with people on *their* turf—in *their* places of work, coffee shops, bars, parks, community centers and gyms. We use what we learn to build bridges of relatability by connecting the dots from the outlandish and hope-filled love of Christ to the heart longings of the people. We learn to ask, "What does the gospel look like to these people in this particular context?"[2]

If the church competes with culture in the relevance game, the church will always lose. Fortunately, that's not our game to play. We have a hopeful message to share, not a cool brand to push onto others. Compassionate hope beats relevant cool every time. And when we lean into our context with a humble missionary posture, we can communicate how the gospel message is "not far from any one of us" (Acts 17:27).

SECTION THREE

Motivation

Talk More About *Coulds* Than *Shoulds*

Bob

Several years ago I spent some time helping a friend who was the young-adult minister at a very conservative Bible church here in Portland. The pastor of the church was a gifted communicator, but a cranky curmudgeon in the pulpit. Week after week I would leave the service understanding the text a little better, but feeling beaten down. Instead of feeling as if the gospel had lifted a weight off my shoulders, I felt as though I had gained a new burden of something I needed to do, or something I needed to do *better*. As I reflected on this, I resolved that the new community I would soon help start would be more about *coulds* than *shoulds*.

Occasionally, we need to *should* people or hear the *shoulds* ourselves; we all need to hear and understand our responsibilities to God, one another and the world. But a steady diet of *shoulds* invariably leads to people who feel dejected and shamed, who feel as if they will never be able to keep up with the growing list of things they need to do, or who see God as someone they will never be able to please. Nobody wants to be around people who are constantly *shoulding* all over themselves.

A steady diet of the gospel—of *coulds*—draws a picture for people of what God wants to do and could do in their lives; it leads people to see their position and acceptance by God based not on what they do, but on what Christ did in his righteous life and atoning death. The *coulds* represent the change that they can partner in with the Holy Spirit and the ways they can be more like

Christ and more free from the sin that so easily entangles. *Coulds* empower, inspire and embolden people to live out the Gospel in their context. *Shoulds* are mainly about keeping standards and toeing the line.

Again, *shoulds* are sometimes necessary, but they should never form the bulk of our communication. Between telling people they can live the kind of life that Jesus lived through the power of the same Holy Spirit and telling people to quit doing what they are doing (and start doing better), it's best to do the former.

This is the approach Paul often took with the church in Corinth (a group that was in need of some *shoulds* if ever there was one!). Paul did tell them what they should do, but his frequent refrain was "I'm not writing this to shame you." When it came time to encourage them to complete the offering they had promised to give to other churches, Paul tells them, "I am not commanding you" to do this (2 Corinthians 8:8). Then he reminds them of God's generosity to them in Christ. It's almost as if he is saying he could order them to do something through his authority as an apostle, but instead, he wants to remind them of God's generosity and let that work into their hearts a generosity toward others.

True righteous living is rarely produced by excoriating sermons or exhorting people week after week to live holy lives. Usually, the best that can produce is an outward conformity and a lot of underground, secret sin. True righteous living comes from gratitude. When people understand all that God has done for them in Christ, and when they begin really to listen to the Spirit of God and respond, radical change flows out of a heart of thanksgiving. The more we meditate on who Jesus is and what he has done for us, the more grateful we become, and the more open we become to what the Spirit may want to do in our lives. Oftentimes, *shoulds* usher in shame, whereas *coulds* provide us with hope.

Which do you think works better in your own heart? As you think about your preaching and teaching, which one do you major in? Don't avoid telling people what they need to hear, but live and lead out of the hope of *coulds* instead of the shame of *shoulds*.

No Matter What, Give Hope

J.R.

Several years ago a team of my friends hosted a counterintuitive event called Epic Fail Pastors Conference. The purpose was to provide hope, healing and encouragement to failed, frustrated, wounded or discouraged pastors.[1] We had invited a recognized Christian leader to the event to present during one of the sessions. His presentation was different from what our planning team had imagined. His tone was sharp, and the topic was quite different from what we told us it would be. What he shared ruffled a lot of feathers. He received a lot of pushback after his presentation—and our planning team received complaints.

A few days after the event, he called to apologize for his remarks and asked me if I thought what he said was out of line. I assured him that I wasn't bothered by the pushback, nor were the complaints from attendees problematic. "But you committed the cardinal sin of leadership," I told him. He was stunned and asked what I meant. "You gave us a lot of things to think about, but you failed to give us hope. No matter what, leaders give hope." There was a long awkward silence on the other end of the phone. "Well, I think you're right. Thanks for the feedback. I'm sorry."

King David, when he was fleeing from his son Absalom, prayed, "But you, Lord, are a shield around me, my glory, *the One who lifts my head high*" (Psalm 3:3; emphasis added). As pastors we are called by God to join him in helping to lift people's heads high. I once heard pastor Dave Gibbons say that the role of a leader is to bear pain and build trust. I really like that, but I'd like to add to it: a leader is one who bears pain, builds trust *and gives hope*. This is how, by the power of God's Spirit, we act as lifters of people's heads. When I bear other people's pain, I am communicating to them that I care, thus building trust. When I build trust with people, I am reminding them of our access to hope. And when I give hope, I am reminding people that the pain they bear is not borne alone or in vain. Leaders are capable of giving all sorts of things to the people we lead, but if we only give people one thing, it must be hope.

Pastor and author John Ortberg wrote, "Nothing kills a ministry or disheartens a pastor like loss of hope. We can endure many losses, but not that one."[2] But this isn't just for pastors; this is for all human beings. The world's most effective leaders know this to be inherently true: *people will only follow someone who offers a compelling vision of hope.*

Paul wrote to the little church in Ephesus: "I pray that the eyes of your heart may be enlightened in order that you may *know the hope to which he has called you*, the riches of his glorious inheritance in his holy people, and his incomparably great power for us who believe" (Ephesians 1:18-19; emphasis mine). Peter, writing to encourage dispersed Christians in five provinces across Asia Minor, said: "Always be prepared to give an answer to everyone who asks you to give the reason for the hope that you have" (1 Peter 3:15).

The good news is that Jesus came to rescue us from our spiritual disappointment. Leaders do soul care for the spiritually disappointed by giving hope. This is not a fantasy hope built on false promises and pithy clichés, but a real, tangible hope found in the power of an empty tomb and a risen Christ. Whether we are sitting with grieving family members at a funeral home, or speaking with a distraught couple in a marriage-counseling session at the office, or preaching a sermon on a Sunday morning, or talking with a neighbor at the mailbox, we're given the awesome responsibility of reminding people of the hope that is available to them through Christ.

Be a lifter of people's heads. Bear pain, build trust and give hope.

If They Know You Love Them, You Can Say Anything to Them

Bob

Love opens doors into people's hearts.

I've devoted a lot of time to studying the life and ministry of seventeenth-century Puritan pastor Richard Baxter. This mantra comes from Baxter's writings.[1] Baxter is known for both his intense pastoral care and his fiery, convicting preaching. He wrote that the key to confronting people with things they might not want to hear, whether it's a general teaching or even personal correction, is *love*.

We're making a deposit of trust every time we show someone pastoral care. We do it without false or ulterior motives; we just need to love the people God has given us to shepherd. But should we ever need to make a withdrawal in the form of a difficult conversation, we know that we have nothing to fear. If they know we love them, we can say anything to them.

It's not necessarily the case that if someone won't listen when confronted, there's been a deficit of love and pastoral care, but it's something to consider. Recently, my copastor Dustin and I confronted someone in our community about how he treated others. The response at first puzzled me: "You haven't provided pastoral care for me!" That seemed like a non sequitur. But the more I thought about it, the more I realized there was some truth there. This person was telling us, in his own way, that he hadn't felt loved enough to receive our constructive feedback and confrontation.

For this reason, when confronting individuals, or when saying hard things to the community as a whole, I try to reaffirm my love for them. But if the first time they hear it is at the actual time of confrontation, it's probably too late.

We ought not shy away from saying the things that need to be said, even if we haven't yet had the opportunity to build a foundation of personal care, but we should think about the foundation we are building—or failing to build—even before we need to have the difficult conversations.

A few years ago I hit choppy waters with one of our staff members. In the midst of the situation, Dustin and another staff member named Devin took me out to a local pub to talk things through, and I realized there were things I needed to own and repent of. It was a difficult conversation, no doubt, but through the process I felt their care and concern—and because of that, I listened to the hard things they needed to say to me. In fact, it may be only because of that that I listened. At the time I felt I was in the right and that they didn't or couldn't see it from my perspective. But the fact that they had banked some significant relational capital with me meant that I was going to hear what they had to say. (Since then, Dustin has continued to tell me on occasion how much he likes me and enjoys working with me—no doubt preparing for the day when he has to confront me once again!)

As a pastor, you have both influence and authority. Lean on influence whenever you can, and pull out the authority card only when it is absolutely needed. Your denominational polity, church constitution, job title, organization chart or congregational structure may give you authority, but only the act of loving people gives you the influence you'll need to have the kinds of conversations that really turn things around for others.

Push—but Don't Shove

J.R.

Have you ever noticed how often Jesus pushes people? Through questions, awkward situations and faith tests, he doesn't let people off the hook very easily.

In John 6 we read about Jesus' purposeful pushing, when he chooses to raise the temperature of expectation and commitment for his disciples. His followers verbalize how difficult his teaching actually is, which prompts Jesus to ask if what he taught them is offensive (see John 6:60-65). A few verses later, the Gospel of John records: "From this time many of his disciples turned back and no longer followed him. 'You do not want to leave too, do you?' Jesus asked the Twelve. Simon Peter answered him, 'Lord, to whom shall we go? You have the words of eternal life. We have come to believe and to know that you are the Holy One of God'" (6:66-69).

Here we see that Jesus pushed people with such intensity that the text says that *many* of his followers left him altogether. Then he turned to the Twelve and challenged them, basically saying, "If you can't stand the heat, get out of the kitchen." When Peter spoke up, he acknowledged the Twelve's commitment—a defining moment in their relationship with their rabbi.

Jesus was full of compassion, but he wasn't soft. Fruitful kingdom leaders are always looking to create high-challenge environments. Just like Jesus, they push people to trust God more, realizing that the closer they follow Jesus, the more he requires of them.

But have you ever noticed that while Jesus pushes people, he doesn't shove them? He doesn't intimidate, manipulate, bully or shame people into following him or doing what he wants them to do. Nobody likes to be shoved. Pushing does not mean leading by manipulation, intimidation or fear. It means challenging people to lean into their unique callings, to trust the Father more deeply, all the while eschewing comfort and ease. Some ministry leaders shove others, veiling their actions in what they call "tough love," but it's nothing more than spiritual bullying and abuse—and it should be stopped immediately.

And yet, for others, the pendulum swings the other way; they leave people alone, allowing them to do what they wish and never challenging them to deeper levels of faith, sacrifice and commitment. They let people stay warmly and safely cocooned in their comfort zones, coddled and enabled. These types of so-called leaders fear they might push people to the point that they might stop giving to, serving or attending the church. That's not leadership; that's appeasement.

Within our church, we work to create leadership structures with three basic distinctions: lightweight, low maintenance and high accountability.[1] This high-accountability posture is something we find all throughout Jesus' ministry.

Clyde and Kim Lehy started attending our church a few years ago. After they had attended for about a month, my copastor Doug took them out for coffee, asking them what they thought of our church and if they had any questions about our community. Clyde replied, "We've felt more uncomfortable here than at any church we've ever been a part of—and we love it. We're being challenged to grow like we haven't been challenged before."

This isn't always the case. We've had other Christian couples visit and leave. When we followed up with these couples, they told us, "Your church challenges people significantly, but we want to find something that makes us feel a little more comfortable." What they were saying is that they didn't want to be challenged and pushed out of their comfort zones. They were looking for a spiritual country club, not a group of people with a white-hot passion who are participating in a revolution of love rooted in God. It might sound harsh, but instead of feeling discouraged by these responses, we were—and are—deeply encouraged that our church's ethos discourages spiritual consumption and refuses to feed the beast of religious consumerism.

What's required in a pushing-but-not-shoving environment is a large dose of wisdom. It also means knowing our people. Jesus said he knew his sheep by name. Certain people respond to challenge differently. Some people's push is another person's shove. We have to understand people, their personalities and how they respond in high-challenge environments. If a leader is a culture cultivator, it's important he or she serves to create a culture that is both high challenge *and* high grace. It should include not legalism or intimidation, but also not letting people off the hook.

Push—but don't shove. Just make sure you push.

SECTION FOUR

Ministry

Ministry Is Meeting People Where They Are and Journeying with Them to Where God Wants Them to Be

J.R.

It was my first class on my first day of my first semester of seminary, and my professor asked a seemingly simple question: "How would you define ministry?" Despite the fact that many of us were in full-time vocational ministry, we had a surprisingly difficult time coming up with a clear, concise and compelling answer. The professor submitted his definition to the class: *ministry is meeting people where they are and journeying with them to where God wants them to be.*

I've pondered and shared this mantra countless times. Not only does this help me define what ministry is, but it also helps me to understand what ministry is not.

Ministry is *not* waiting for people to come to us and journeying with them to where God wants them to be. That's an antiquated paradigm that worked in past generations, but not in our current post-Christian context.

Ministry is *not* meeting people where they are and being content with staying where they are. That's friendship (better yet, acquaintanceship), but it's not ministry.

Ministry is *not* meeting people where they are and journeying with them to where I want them to be. That's not ministry; that's manipulation.

Ministry is *not* meeting people where they are and journeying with them to where they want to be. That's probably just Oprah . . . with a little bit of Jesus sprinkled in.

Ministry is *not* a mindset of, as the baseball movie *Field of Dreams* made popular, "if you build it they will come."

Bishop Graham Cray, archmissioner of the global mission-aligned movement Fresh Expressions, describes incarnational ministry as threefold: we enter their world, we take it as seriously as they do and we help them find Christ—who's already there.[1] Simply, we go to them.

Healthy churches have this deeply embedded into their DNA. They realize ministry is primarily *out there*, rather than *in here*. Certainly, our Sunday gatherings have a significant place in the life of the local church; but in healthy churches it is clearly understood what role Sunday gatherings play, and what role they do not. This definition of ministry carries the conviction that God's Spirit is actively at work *in the entire process,* from start to finish. We don't do this in our own power; the Spirit initiates, prepares, invites, instructs and guides. It is in the power of the Spirit that all ministry happens.

When we were in the early formative stages of planting our church, I shared this ministry mantra with our core team. The challenge was to live out ministry in our everyday lives in the boardroom, the classroom, the playroom, the family room and the schoolroom—*out there.* We did not want to create a huddle-and-cuddle culture of church. We made a weekly practice of allowing space for people to hear God stories. Each Sunday we would share how God was actively at work, how he was using us when we made ourselves accessible to the Spirit. We shared with joy where we had joined with God in obedience—and confessed openly where we had resisted him. Our team realized that church only makes sense on Sunday if it's lived out Monday through Saturday. We've always believed that

Sunday is not the game; it's the pep rally. The pep rally is important, but it exists to prepare us for the game ahead.

To this day, we devote about ten minutes in each of our Sunday gatherings for a Time of Story. We invite one or two people to share how they are joining with God in the Monday-through-Saturday reality of their lives. We don't ask them to share ancient history ("I became a Christian when I was six, and I've been in church ever since . . .") but what's happening *right now,* in this season of their lives. Sometimes it's dramatic and inspiring, but most of the time the stories are simple acts of obedience to the Spirit. For example, the young adult who made a commitment to lovingly and humbly meet those far from God on their turf, which opened up doors of opportunity to engage with the God of the Universe. Or, the stay-at-home mom who moved from being resentful that she had to give up her career to raise her children to learning to pray for the other stay-at-home moms on her street—and then ultimately inviting them to her home to listen to, love and pray with and for them.

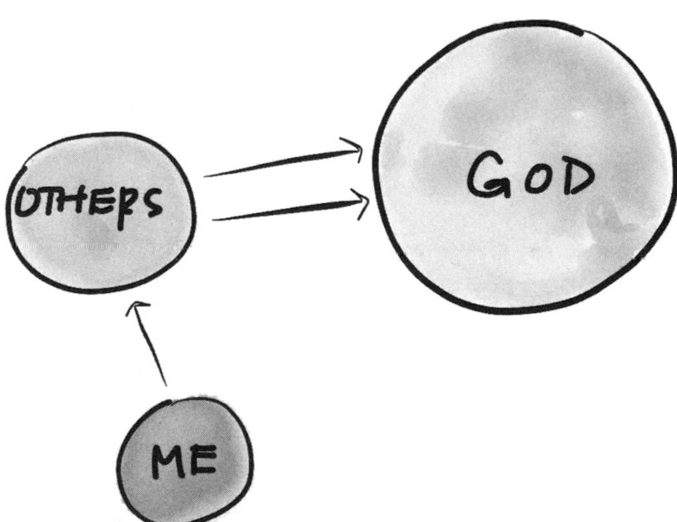

Or, the high school junior trying to live with integrity when the temptations for compromise abound in his school. Or, the car salesman praying for his customers as children of God, and not as people to earn commission.

Ministry happens when God's people meet others where they are and journey with them in the direction of God's heart.

Ministry Happens in the Interruptions

J.R.

Why is it that the most significant ministry opportunities seem to happen at the most inconvenient times?

As a driven, focused, goal-oriented leader with a disciplined personality, interruptions are difficult for me. They throw off the schedule, change plans, add to my growing to-do list and add stress. In those rare moments of clarity when I can step back, take a deep breath and trust God's sovereignty, I'm able to whisper, "All right God, I'm available. Where can I be accessible to you and others right now?" Admittedly, these moments are too rare for me. It's why I have to repeat this mantra to myself. Interruption-laden ministry is truly inefficient; however, it is undoubtedly effective.

Jesus' most powerful encounters with people happened during the spontaneous moments, punctuated by desperation, surprise or inconvenience. Wine runs out at Cana. A sinful woman barges in and wipes Jesus' feet with her tears and hair. Jesus turns around and heals a loud blind man as he's leaving Jericho. But Jesus' encounter with the daughter of the synagogue official Jairus is most striking (see Mark 5). Jesus is *interrupted from his interruption from his interruption*. The interruptions come from the swarming crowd, the bumbling disciples, a chronically bleeding woman and mourners who stopped their grieving and laughed at Jesus. And yet it's in the interruptions that powerful ministry occurs.

Jesus even told stories that involved interruptions. The good Samaritan's schedule and cultural customs are interrupted. The shepherd is interrupted by a wandering sheep and leaves the ninety-nine others to find it. The parable of the prodigal son involves many interruptions, including the ears, hearts and minds of the religious elite—and our own definition of which son we believe is the real prodigal.

Interruptions are a given in ministry. The text from an anxious mother about her teenager at 11:30 p.m. The phone call at 2:00 a.m. that requires getting up and driving to the hospital to visit a congregant. The sudden illness of your worship leader late Saturday night. The couple whose marital problems are so severe that they need to come over to the house now, even though you had plans for a quiet night at home with your spouse. The crisis that blows up two hours before your family is scheduled to pull out of the driveway to start vacation.

Ministry seems to happen at all the wrong times.

When I'm frustrated by these realities, it's because I believe that the person standing in front of me in need of help is an interruption. But I am most effective in ministry when I realize the interruption in front of me is a person with a real need who is in need of real hope.

I once read about a pastor who was interrupted frequently from his responsibilities. Instead of becoming frustrated, he would smile and say calmly, "Please, come sit down and let's figure out why God had our two paths cross today." This receptive, patient, Spirit-directed posture is a mark of anticipatory ministry.

As stated elsewhere, ministry is meeting people where they are and journeying with them to where God wants them to be. Journeying with people doesn't fit into sixty-minute slots scheduled tidily on our calendars. In fact, many times it happens at what feels like the absolute worst times. Yet sometimes, when we are capable of seeing through the lens of the kingdom, we may realize that in those situations of inconvenience, we may be the ones being ministered to.

You can't plan for interruptions, but you can prepare for them. And when they come, see them as people to be loved and not problems to be fixed.

What You Win Them With Is What You Win Them To

Bob

Every Easter, every Christmas—no, scratch that—*every Sunday*, we as leaders are faced with a dilemma: Do we go big, advertise, put on an amazing show and attract people who otherwise wouldn't have visited? Or do we simply remain a faithful gospel presence, observing the important days of the Christian calendar, but avoiding any hint of spectacle? Can we trust the work of the Holy Spirit and the good reputation of a community of love to draw those who come?

What we win people *with* is what we win them *to*. Those who are drawn in by the smoke machines, the amazing technical productions or even the polished preaching of the quasi-celebrity Christian voice tend to stick around as long as those things remain available—or until they learn of another church doing it a little bit better.

Those drawn in by the reality and closeness of Christian community through love and radical hospitality don't tend to be pulled away by other things. They've tasted the reality of church community and don't feel the allure of smoke and mirrors. To be clear, I'm not condemning "excellence," but I do question its priority at some churches. Is the reality of the presence of Christ among a people of love, inviting us to worship together as we gather around his table, no longer enough? Now, the music has to be louder, the sermon funnier and more engaging, the weekly activities bigger and better. There need to be a lot more exclamation points on our websites and mailings.

I've wondered what the people who start attending churches during the Advent or Easter seasons think as the spectacle dies down and things return to normal. Do they wonder what happened to all the production, the huge effort they saw expended? Do they feel caught in the middle of an ecclesiastical bait and switch? I would.

I never want to find myself on the hamster wheel of church performance, trying to outdo the church down the street or even trying to outdo what we ourselves did last week. Our staff sometimes jokes that if we ever find ourselves renting a helicopter in order to rain down prize-stuffed Easter eggs on a crowd, we'll know we've taken a wrong turn somewhere.

We want people to connect with our communities, but we have to want them to do so for the right reasons. I just don't buy the "anything to win souls" mindset, especially when I see churches giving away cars, houses and even, in more than one case, AR-15 rifles to entice people to attend church. If you want to give away things, then give them in the love of Christ, without making a not-so-subtle play to boost attendance. Generosity is something we do in response to the gospel, not as a ploy to raise attendance.

If you want to draw people to your community, let the community itself (its love and unity and gospel ethos) be the draw, not the efforts expended by a small team of people to draw a crowd. Anyone can draw a crowd—but it takes partnering with the Holy Spirit to build a *community*.

How Matters

J.R.

The Puritans had a wonderful mantra: "God loveth adverbs." God cares about the way in which we do things, even the little things. The right thing done the wrong way can easily become the wrong thing. *How* we do things matters to God and to other people. 1 Corinthians 13 reminds us we can do great things, but when they are done absent of love, they are nothing.

Why is it that the more right we think we are, the less kind we think we have to be? It's a question I've wrestled with for many years. Oftentimes we believe our rightness justifies our meanness.

The Scriptures emphasize how things should be done. Jesus says that if you do it to the least of these, you do it to me (see Matthew 25:40). He praises a woman who gives a few coins at the temple treasury—not because of the amount, but because she gave out of the little she had (see Luke 21:1-4). In the Sermon on the Mount, Jesus says when you pray, go into your closet and do it secretly. When you give, don't let others see it. When you fast, don't tell others about it (see Matthew 6:1-18).

Jesus tells his followers and the crowd listening: "The teachers of the law and the Pharisees sit in Moses' seat. So you must be careful to do everything they tell you. But do not do what they do, for they do not practice what they preach" (Matthew 23:2-3). *What* they tell you is good, but *how* they do it is wrong. Their *how* is off. Notice that Jesus assumes that what we will do—praying, fasting and giving—is a given. But he redirects people in their inner motivations.

In any situation, it's wise to ask: "What is my motive? Am I doing this to impress others and make myself look good? Am

I doing this cheerfully or begrudgingly? Am I doing this out of a legalistic 'should-do' or a grace-filled response?" If the internal *how* is off, it can spoil my external *what.* Jesus called incongruent people hypocrites.

In sixth grade the Christian school I attended required students to take Latin. I don't remember much from my Latin class; in fact, I despised it. Looking back, I should've paid attention much more than I did. However, on the first day of class Mrs. Hogan walked to the chalkboard and wrote out Colossians 3:23: "Whatever you do, work at it with all your heart, as working for the Lord, not for human masters." Our first assignment of the school year was to memorize that verse. It's come to mind hundreds of times since—and I will forever be grateful for Mrs. Hogan's assignment. It has reoriented how I do things and how I approach things—the motivation of my own heart.

Jesus cared more about motivations and affections than external behaviors—because *how* matters.

The Essence of Discipleship Is Not Knowledge, but Imitation

J.R.

If you ever see me in a coffee shop meeting with someone, chances are you'll see a black hardcover Moleskine notebook on the table in front of me. I carry it with me just about everywhere I go. It includes diagrams, thoughts and helpful resources that I readily share with other leaders any chance I get. My friends have dubbed it my "discipleship notebook."

I have yet to meet a healthy church that does not take discipleship seriously. Because of this, I have made a lifelong commitment to learn not only what discipleship is but also to learn how best to communicate and embody it among those who are hungry to know more about entering into and living out the Way of Jesus.

The most significant misconception about discipleship is that it is simply knowledge acquisition. Intellectual transmission is not the same as spiritual formation. If this notion is left unchallenged, it can have damaging results.

A disciple is one who desires—above all else—to be like Jesus and then arranges his or her life to be like him. We can be spiritual and religious—we can even be believers—but that doesn't guarantee that we are disciples of Jesus. Ministry leaders are the ones called to steward the opportunity for a group of people to organize and align their lives around the person of Jesus. It is, as Dallas Willard says, the process of "learning from him how to lead my life as he would lead my life if he were I."[1]

The test of all teaching is practice. The onus is on us to preach a gospel that will actually make disciples. Discipleship is rooted in *concrete actions and practices*, not just the transfer of information. Jesus' lessons weren't in classrooms, but on field trips. Believing something simply is not enough. Jesus told his disciples that the fruit of our lives will reveal whether we are his disciples or not (see John 13:34-35; 15). The fruits reveal the roots. Discipleship is not primarily cognitive, but experiential.

Many people *like* Jesus, but that's quite different from committing to trust Christ and organizing our lives around the story of Jesus. Discipleship is an active movement toward Jesus that is visible to all and contains concrete behaviors.

The true test of the church is the quality and quantity of its disciples, people who are apprentices of Jesus and actually trying to live out what he said. Therefore, instead of teaching on prayer for thirty-five minutes, it might be more effective to teach on prayer for ten or fifteen minutes and then to allow twenty minutes for prayer together. True disciples don't simply *know about* the kingdom of God; they choose to submit to it, and therefore experience it firsthand.

In order for people to understand discipleship as beyond knowledge acquisition, we have to possess a deep commitment to develop people to be lovers of God, followers of Jesus and listeners of the Spirit. Teach people to live it out, not just learn about it.

Focus on Who People Are Becoming

J.R.

Near my house is a wellness center called The Becoming Center. Each time I drive by the sign I can't help but ask, "What if churches saw themselves as 'becoming centers'?"

It can be easy to forget that our identity as Christ followers isn't to be found in what we do or how well we do it, but in who we are and who we are becoming. Who we are becoming is the most important thing about us. Discipleship is a process, not something we arrive at successfully. Oftentimes when we're tempted to look at numbers in our churches—focusing only on buildings, bodies and budgets—we can see people as commodities. Nobody wants to be used. As pastors we must be careful not to use people to accomplish our own goals and visions.

Some push back on this idea: "But what about calling them to a decision for Christ? Are you saying that doesn't matter?" Consider this: in the Gospel accounts, when did Peter become a Christian? Was it when Jesus said to follow him, and he'll make him a fisher of men? Was it in Mark 8, when Jesus asked him who he thought Jesus was, and he responded by saying he was the Christ? Was it after he had denied Jesus three times, or when Jesus restored him after his resurrection? Or was it years later, when he could process all of who Jesus was, and was ultimately willing to risk his life for Christ? No answer can be given with absolute certainty. What we do know is that, at times, Peter (along with the other disciples) stumbled, tripped, crawled and fell flat on his face—but he stumbled in the direction of Christ.

It's worth wondering: "Who am I becoming?" May we never forget that God is not only working through us; he is also working in us. We are always a work in progress. As followers of Jesus, we never fully arrive this side of heaven.

Focusing on who people are becoming means focusing on growing hearts and not on growing numbers. In our church we're always looking for leaders—regardless of talent or level of expertise—who are F.A.T. (Faithful, Available and Teachable). If we can find leaders who are faithful to God, to others and to their commitments; who are available and accessible; and who possess a teachable and humble spirit, we're convinced God can use them. Spiritual leaders, regardless of their skills, experience and passion, who are arrogant, self-reliant, unteachable or lacking compassion are unqualified to lead.

As leaders ourselves, we also must become the kind of spiritual leaders who are more interested in being spiritual directors than program directors. We must be F.A.T. leaders, too.

In this vein, we ask the people in our church frequently—in our gatherings, one-on-one and in small-group settings—"In God's power and grace, what would have to happen for you to be closer to Jesus in six months than you are right now? What would you have to let go of?"

Are the people in your church leaning in the direction of Jesus or leaning away? Are they concerned about becoming like Jesus in their everyday lives? These questions will assist you in cultivating Jesus-centered "becoming centers" known as local churches.

Remember, the Vegetables Aren't Ready Yet

J.R.

As a pastor I'm embarrassed by my level of impatience. Several years ago one Mother's Day afternoon, my oldest son, who was three at the time, wanted to help my wife start the seeding for our small, backyard vegetable garden. He put on his gardening boots and gloves and, with trowel in hand, waddled out to help for a few minutes until I called him in to wash up and go down for a nap. Later that afternoon, I heard him waking up and went upstairs to greet him. When I walked into his room, he opened his eyes, sat up and asked with all earnestness, "Are the vegetables ready yet, Daddy?"

I chuckled at the childish naïveté. "No, buddy. That's not how vegetables work. It takes a long time. The vegetables will take several weeks before they will even poke their little green heads up out of the soil—and even more time before they grow large enough for us to eat." He was dejected.

But don't I have the same mindset in ministry? It's easy to ask, "Are the vegetables ready yet?" Oftentimes the answer is a definitive no. We pour our lives into others, oftentimes going months, years—sometimes decades—before seeing any tangible fruit from our faithful investment.

As Eugene Peterson writes—quoting German philosopher Friedrich Nietzsche—a life committed to ministry is a "long obedience in the same direction."[1] Much of ministry is learning to plod along faithfully, even when we aren't seeing "results." We can become disappointed when we don't see anything poking up through the soil—especially when the neighbor's vegetables are waist-high.

I've coached many pastors with sagging shoulders, diverted eyes and lowered volume who tell me they've been investing in people for years and are left wondering if it's made any ounce of difference. I encourage them to keep plodding, keep cultivating healthy soil, keep watering. The vegetables aren't ready yet. But it's worth the effort.

Kent, an IT specialist and a key leader at our church, and his wife, Cindy, have given of themselves tirelessly to the work of the kingdom. They open their home to others for meals. Several years ago they joined a local community theater in order to build relationships with local actors and actresses who are far from Christ. Recently, Kent was elected president of the theater because of the trust he's built through his compassionate presence. Additionally, Kent and Cindy joined a ballroom-dancing class simply to build relationships with people far from Christ. Eventually they were asked to take over the class when the teacher retired. Every Wednesday and Friday morning, Kent eats breakfast at the same greasy-spoon diner and bar for bikers to build trusted relationships through consistent presence. One evening when he was offered drugs, he offered the drug dealer Christ's love. They've shared their faith with couples after dance class, and have compassionately listened to lonely patrons who come and hang out at the restaurant because they don't know where else to go. They've prayed in the parking lot with and for local actors after rehearsals.

But the difficult part for Kent and Cindy is, despite years of sacrificial ministry and faith-filled prayer for God to do something significant in people's spiritual realities, there's been little evidence of fruit. Many times over omelets and coffee, I've reminded Kent to keep scattering seed and not give up. Oftentimes I encourage him by simply saying, "It seems the vegetables just aren't ready yet."

Keep plodding.

Keep scattering seed.

The vegetables don't seem to be ready yet.

And remember: it's still worth the effort.

Pay Attention to God, and Respond Appropriately

J.R.

"So, what do you do?"

It's a question I get asked frequently when I travel. I'm presented with two options. I can either be honest, or I can be *creatively* honest. Thus, my answers differ. If I want to sleep or get some work done, I usually say, "I'm a pastor." As other pastors know, when uttering the *p*-word I get all sorts of reactions. But most are polite and awkward. Usually the conversation ends shortly thereafter. From my experience I've found that people are afraid of making small talk with pastors.

But if I sense there is an opportunity to talk to this person in meaningful conversation, I respond by saying, "I'm a Practical and Educational Theologist." The response is usually the same: they look at me curiously and usually say something like, "Wow, I've never heard of a position like that before. What exactly does that entail?" I tell them that while the title may sound impressive, my job—and my life—is devoted to helping people pay attention to God and respond appropriately. They usually ask follow-up questions about what an average week looks like or about how I first became interested in this field. But on occasion, after a few minutes, they look at me with narrowed eyes and a smirk and ask, "Wait. Are you a pastor?"

"Some call me that," I usually say with a wink.

That phrase "helping people pay attention to God and respond appropriately" is one that I've picked up from Eugene Peterson, who's been a mentor of mine for almost my entire ministry. Several years ago I was invited to visit with him and his wife, Jan, at their lakefront home in Montana for a few days. One afternoon, on a hike in the crisp June air, I asked Eugene, "There are volumes of books written about the pastorate. But what *exactly* is the role of a pastor in the life of the congregation? How would you define it briefly?" He looked up and said succinctly, "It's to help people pay attention to God and respond appropriately." I was so struck by his response that it changed the way I do ministry. Every week I ask myself, "Is what I am doing helping others pay attention to what God is doing and saying, and am I encouraging, challenging, praying and urging people to respond appropriately and obediently with their lives?"

Peterson articulates this idea slightly differently in the introduction to his book *Working the Angles,* where he writes:

> The biblical fact is that there are no successful churches. There are, instead, communities of sinners, gathered before God week after week in towns and villages all over the world. The Holy Spirit gathers them and does his work in them. In these communities of sinners, one of the sinners is called pastor and given a designated responsibility in the community. The pastor's responsibility is to keep the community attentive to God.[1]

Our Greek word for church—*ekklēsia*—finds its root in *kaleō*—"to call out." The *ekklēsia*, the church, is therefore "the called-out ones." When the *ekklēsia* is being faithful, we are hearing God's Spirit call out to us, and we are responding appropriately, faithfully and obediently to his voice, both individually and communally.

Oftentimes we can pay attention to God but respond inappropriately. Jonah seems to be a poignant example. He knew *exactly* what God was asking him to do—he just chose to run in the complete opposite direction (see Jonah 1:1-3). Other times we have trouble paying attention and thus don't know how to respond faithfully. Young Samuel, called by God in the middle of the night, but believing he had heard the voice of Eli, is a good example of this (see 1 Samuel 3:1-17). Samuel needed the guidance and wisdom of the priest Eli (despite his shortcomings and failings as a leader) to help guide him to pay attention to the Lord's voice in order to respond appropriately. Eli's life and ministry remind us that we must lead by our own example. We must pay attention to God and respond appropriately in our own lives first, or we have no pastoral integrity or authority with which to lead.

When ministry gets complex—through new programs, a half dozen new meetings landing on the schedule, a myriad of emails and phone calls to return, or hospital visits to make—let us never forget that our primary responsibility and calling as ministers of the gospel is to help people pay attention to God and respond appropriately. And it must start with us first.

Ask the Right Questions at the Right Time to the Right People for the Right Reason

J.R.

Have you ever noticed how often Jesus asked questions? I'm utterly fascinated by questions and committed to being a lifelong student of the art of asking questions. Questions are a gift to people. Leaders aren't often accused of being good listeners or of being good at asking questions. Yet so much of Jesus' effectiveness in ministry was borne out of his ability to ask direct questions of great significance.

I have facilitated an exercise with a roomful of ministry leaders on several occasions where I ask, "What did Jesus do?" As people respond, I write their answers on a whiteboard or flip chart. Common answers are that he healed, forgave, taught, discipled, saved, died and rose again, told parables, performed miracles, slept, got upset at the religious leaders, and cared for the poor. All of these answers are true. Yet in all the times I've led these exercises, not once has someone mentioned that Jesus asked questions. Jesus is Savior, Lord, King, teacher, healer and rabbi, but he is also a question-asker.

Jesus asked a lot of questions in the Gospels—307 to be exact. He is asked 183 questions. *And yet he only directly answered three of them.*[1] Jesus not only knew what questions to ask, but he knew *who* to ask, *when* to ask—and even *where* to ask them. Jesus' ministry through questions has gone largely unnoticed and underappreciated. We would be all the wiser to study and learn from him as the brilliant question-asker. If our aim as disciple-making disciples is to be like Jesus—and Jesus frequently asked truthful, significant, compassionate and incisive questions—should we not be committed to learning to do the same?

Whether in formal teaching settings, group discussions, parties, confrontational meetings or one-on-one encounters over coffee, questions are the secret sauce of ministry. Certainly, Jesus used far more than questions in his teaching ministry. He spoke truth declaratively when it needed to be communicated. But oftentimes his use of questions—most notably, rhetorical questions—cracked open the door to numerous ministry opportunities.

- Who do people say I am? What about you—who do you say I am? (Mark 8:27, 29)
- Which is easier: to say, "Your sins are forgiven," or to say, "Get up and walk"? (Matthew 9:5)
- What is the kingdom of God like? (Luke 13:18)
- What is your name? (Mark 5:9)
- What do you want me to do for you? (Mark 10:51)
- Do you want to get well? (John 5:6)

The world sees church leaders all too eager to talk. Indeed, proclaiming the good news is needed. But Jesus didn't always walk into towns and villages and start preaching. He asked a lot of questions. Questions have a way of building trust, developing dialogue and pulling in listeners to participate in what is being said—even to confound, confuse and infuriate others. Questions also have a way of engaging people by communicating value, trust, respect and dignity.

Imagine if ministry leaders were known more for our incisive questions than for our brilliant answers. How might opportunities for ministry increase if we were to grow in our ability to ask significant questions?

If we were to do so, how might the current perception of the church be different?

What questions are we currently asking?

And how might we learn to give answers less and ask questions more?

What if we were to be known more by leading with our ears than with our mouths?

SECTION FIVE

Pastoral Care

Don't Wonder When You Can Just Ask

Bob

"Why did he do that?" "What do they need from us?" "Did we hurt them somehow?" These are all questions I've heard at our leadership-team meetings. They are ones I'm sure you've heard asked as well, or at least ones like them.

In another mantra, we will encourage you to let your community know that you can't read minds, and so they should let their needs be known. This mantra is a corollary: you can't read minds, so don't try. Don't wonder when you can just ask.

We as leaders often have a strange aversion to the direct approach. It's almost as though knowledge that is acquired through simply asking people what they meant by something or what they might need from us is less valuable than knowledge that we intuit. In a way, that's just pride working in us. We want to be the people who figure it out. Or perhaps, we're afraid to look like the people who don't know and so have to ask. Either way, I know when I find myself wondering why people are doing something, or what they meant by something they said, it's usually pride that is keeping me from just asking.

As leaders, this is particularly dangerous. Too much hurt comes from the kind of misunderstandings that arise when we act or make decisions with a less-than-clear picture of a situation. Assuming you know why someone left your church, assuming you know why someone made a hurtful comment, assuming you understand someone's motivation in opposing something you'd like to do in ministry—all without ever asking—is a recipe for ministry disaster. Proverbs 2:3 urges us: "Call out for insight and cry aloud for understanding." As we read that, most of us probably assume the writer intends that we would cry out to God for the wisdom we need. But the question is, why cry out to God alone, when we can also ask the person about whom we are wondering? Certainly we should seek wisdom from God, but why not also ask the people directly involved what's going on?

J.R. asks a great question in another chapter: "What if we were to be known more by leading with our ears than with our mouths?" It's a wonderfully insightful question. As leaders we have to fight the temptation to speak first and listen later. I've had to fight my own tendency to see every problem as simply part of a category: all marital issues the same, all church squabbles the same, all staff tension the same. Our longing to understand and simplify things can lead us to assume we understand a situation just because we've seen something somewhat like it in the past. But of course, the similarities are only surface level. And only good, deep questions will clear away the surface level and allow us to see, hear and understand what's really going on down below.

I know that this mantra seems like common sense. But I also know from my own time in ministry that there can be a shyness about asking people questions that might seem obtrusive as they deal with heart motivations and often questionable actions. For their sake, and for yours, learn not to make assumptions, and get past the fear or pride that may keep you from asking. Don't wonder when you can just ask.

If You Are Available to Everyone, You Are Available to No One

Bob

We had one person attending our church who always wanted to see me *now.* Too often I heard, "I'm in the midst of a crisis right now, and I have some time this afternoon. In fact, I'm driving over that way right now. Do you have some time?" This person singlehandedly forced me to begin screening my calls. Dealing with several people like this at the same time left me worn out, unable to give my best to anyone else.

The reality of ministry is that your supply of availability is often exceeded by the amount of people and demands on your time. And if you are available to everyone, all the time, you will be spread so thin that you are *effectively* available to no one.

Over the last few years I've begun to protect my days off and evenings much more purposefully, and I try not to have church-related activities or meetings more than one or two nights a week. My family needs me more than the folks at church do. Here's how I prioritize my ministry time.

First, I address people who are present who both want and need pastoral attention. These are people who show up consistently and are present to the community. When they need and want pastoral care and attention, they get it. And I'm not talking about just people who "serve." Mainly I'm talking pure presence. Are you there? Do you show up to events and gatherings and allow yourself to be known and to get to know others?

Second, I address people who are present who need but don't want pastoral attention. This may cover people in crisis, people who are acting out, or people who need a helpful pastoral kick in the seat. They may not be asking for my attention, at least overtly, but part of being one of their pastors is being present to them in these times.

Third, I address people who are present who want but don't need pastoral attention. They tie with the next group in my mind, but these are people who show up consistently, who are present to the community, who contribute in really positive ways, and who want some of my attention. I'm happy to give it to them provided I have some.

Fourth, I address people who are not present who don't want but do need pastoral attention. I try to balance that last group with this one. People who are drifting away, maybe because of crisis, maybe because they are not giving their relationship with God the care and nurture it needs—we want to pursue these folks and let them know that they are missed and that we are available. If I sense it's more of a "fit" thing with our community, and they are finding community elsewhere, obviously I let that go. But when it's a matter of someone wandering off from the flock, I absolutely want to make that effort.

Finally, I address people who are not present and don't need but do want pastoral attention. If you haven't already gotten one, you may soon receive what we have come to refer to affectionately as "pastoral booty calls." These come from people who stopped being a part of your community a while ago, who have no intention of reengaging with community, but who haven't found anyone else to pay attention to them, so they give you a call wanting to have coffee. Feel free to say no. The temptation will be to schedule these people for a couple weeks from now when your schedule looks a bit freer. But believe me—by the time you actually get there, the people from higher up on your taxonomy will *need* your time and you will have guilt and shame for having scheduled this appointment when there are real needs that require attending to.

Clearly, I write about some of this lightly, but these are *people.* There are times when the Holy Spirit gives you, the pastor or ministry leader, a nudge, and you make room for someone for whom you might otherwise not, "just because." Or maybe you want to make a renewed effort with someone. It's a matter of discernment, not a hard and fast rule.

Not everyone who asks for your time should get it—or get it in equal amounts. As a pastor, you are *not* able to practice "first come, first served." Your role in your community and the calling on your life are too important not to think through how and with whom you spend your time. If you are available to everyone, you are available to no one.

Learn the Difference Between *To* and *For*

Bob

Prepositions make a huge difference.

If there's one mantra that I've seen make the most difference for the pastors I get to coach and occasionally teach at church-planter functions and other events, it's this one. I see the impact immediately in their faces as they begin to understand what it is I'm talking about. And I've seen the difference in their lives as they begin to put it into practice.

To put it simply, you as a pastor or ministry leader are not responsible *for* anyone in your community or under your care. This may go against much of what you have been taught or what you feel in ministry, but believe me—it's true.

You have responsibilities *to* your people—real, serious, weighty responsibilities. But you are not responsible *for* them. The weight of their marriages does not rest on your shoulders. Their decisions to follow or not to follow Christ are not up to you. The choices they make, whether good or bad, are their own. Your job is to love them radically, to preach the gospel to them compellingly, to pray for them passionately and to represent Christ to them faithfully. Then, your responsibility is to leave the outcomes up to God.

Letting go of outcomes is one of the hardest things you can do as a kingdom leader. We live in a culture that is driven by outcomes; we measure them, talk about them, dream about them and obsess over them. And yet an outcome is the one thing that remains stubbornly beyond our control. We simply cannot make people respond to and follow Jesus. We cannot make them be faithful to their spouses or make good choices, and we cannot make them grow spiritually.

What we can do is discharge the responsibilities we have to them faithfully, place the results in God's hands and then get a good night's sleep. Before I really grabbed hold of this, I lost many a night's sleep worrying over the people in my community and the courses they were charting for their lives. I would wake up in the middle of the night suddenly reminded that someone hadn't been around in a while, wondering how they were doing spiritually and, of course, what I needed to do to get them back on track. It drove me to pray for them, but it also drove me to insomnia. Eventually I had to realize that the only person I am truly responsible for, because the only person I *can* be responsible for, is myself.

As I began to grapple with this, reminding myself often of the difference between *to* and *for*, I began to find a lot more freedom in ministry. Of course, I still grieve when people choose to walk away from the faith or from marriages, but I've found the ability not to feel personally responsible when they do. I've been able to stop playing the "what if?" game with myself, no longer second-guessing every interaction with them as though somehow I was the reason they chose as they chose or did as they did.

My focus has become getting my prepositional posture right. Am I really giving them the straight truth? Do I preach the gospel faithfully and do my best to make skillful application to life today? Am I appropriately available to people? Do I reach out pastorally when I sense there may be trouble, or even when someone just hasn't been around in a while? And most importantly, do I pray for our people, seeking to know what's happening in their lives so I can pray more precisely for them? When I have done these things, I know I have fulfilled my responsibilities to my church community and can leave the outcomes in God's hands. And I get a good night's sleep, too.

SECTION SIX

Leadership Development

They May Be Your 80, but They're Probably Someone Else's 20

Bob

The 80/20 principle holds that 80 percent of the work in your church will be done by 20 percent of the people. It's one of the most enduring pieces of conventional wisdom in church leadership.

As a young pastor, I had big dreams of turning that principle on its head. My desire was to see 100 percent of our people pitching in and helping, or at least 80 percent, while perhaps the other 20 percent would be people who were recovering from bad church experiences elsewhere or otherwise healing.

A number of things changed my mind about this—the first thing being reality. It just wasn't realistic to assume that anything like 100 percent of people or even 80 percent would be regular, active volunteers. The second thing was realizing I didn't really want that.

One of the big light-bulb moments I had as we pushed for greater involvement and ownership in our community (and I do believe we have well over 20 percent who are active volunteers in our church) was that many people who were a part of our "80" (those not signing up to do much) were mostly all doing really great things elsewhere. They were involved in neighborhood associations or nonprofits doing good work in the city, or they were actively helping their neighbors—in other words, they were a part of someone else's 20.

There's one guy in our church community who used to lead worship and play guitar in the band pretty regularly. He hasn't done much of that over the last couple of years, and I'm glad. Not because he wasn't good at it (because he was), but because he's been busy starting America's first nonprofit brew pub. He had a dream to start a business where all the profits were given to local organizations that were working hard to make the world a better place, and he went for it. Combine that passion with his love of brewing beer and Portland's love of drinking beer, and you have a potent source for doing good in the world. We lost a worship leader, but we, and our city, gained so much more in return.

As you look out over your congregation, you may see a lot of people who aren't doing much in your church. Before you chastise them or begin devising schemes to get more people to volunteer for more things, take some time and find out what people *are* doing. Whether through conversations or surveys, figure out who, while technically part of the 80 percent in your church, are on the front lines elsewhere, working hard for the kingdom, pouring themselves out for the greater good. And then celebrate them. Point them out. Resist the urge to feel that if it's not done for your church, or under your leadership, then it doesn't count.

Don't just honor the volunteers in your kids ministry or worship ministry—honor *everyone* who is giving his or her time and talents to others.

Don't Do for the Community What They Ought to Be Doing for Themselves

Bob

One of the most difficult elements for a leader to cultivate in a culture is a sense of *active passivity.* When we notice a lack, or someone brings a need in the community to our attention, our first instinct is almost always to add the item to our ever-growing to-do list and fix the problem ourselves. Or maybe, if we're swamped, we'll hand it off to someone else on staff (who also has his or her own ever-growing list of things to do).

While I think that there are things that can and ought to be handled by the pastors, elders or other leaders of a church, I think the vast majority of things that come up fit into the category of things we ought to take an actively passive stance on—that is, things about which we intentionally do nothing, and see what others are willing to step up and do.

Perhaps I shouldn't say "do nothing," because one thing we should definitely do, if we're trying to avoid doing for the community what they ought to be doing for themselves, is to point (publicly, repeatedly) at the problem and let people know it exists. Some may have already noticed it and have been wondering when you were going to fix it. Others may be blissfully unaware. But in pointing at the problem, you are laying the responsibility squarely in their laps and asking them to fix it.

More, you are training the community to take initiative and be proactive. Sure, if someone steps up and says he or she wants to help, you may need to do some coaching behind the scenes to help that person accomplish what he or she wants to do. But in doing this, you are fulfilling the role of an equipper, and giving up the role of an enabler. An equipper helps other people to do what needs to be done. An enabler does it for them. Where this begins to get real is when we move beyond the question, "Who's going to take care of coffee on Sunday morning?" and into more mission-critical questions such as "What are we going to do for kids on Sunday morning?"

I first heard that latter question, during one of our initial core team meetings before we even launched our Sunday gathering. I already knew that in order to survive as a pastor, I couldn't be in charge of everything. But as the weeks wore on, the list of things I could see people looking to me to be in charge of solving was growing and growing. So, when that question was asked, I simply turned it around and said, "I don't know—what are *we* going to do for kids?" What followed was a great, formative discussion that began to lay the stage for what we wanted to see happen for children in our community. I'm so glad I didn't offer to get back to them with a five-point plan for children's ministry. I'm so glad I refused to do the work for them that they could and should do for themselves.

When kids' ministry did eventually get off the ground in our community, the reality was that it took a good amount of behind-the-scenes coaching, not just from me, but also from other folks in our community who actually had experience in that area. But the lay-driven nature of what we developed really stuck. It wasn't till year nine or ten that the ministry grew to a complexity that we had to hire someone part-time to oversee things. Of course, it was someone already in our community who was passionate about what we were doing for kids, knew well what we had done in the past and had great ideas for where we needed to go.

Not doing for your community what they can and should do for themselves may cost you—in the early years, before things really developed, we had a lot of folks come and go who loved our community but wanted more for their kids. I certainly sympathized, as I have children of my own. But continuing to point at the need while refusing to solve it myself led to an outburst of creativity and ownership in our community that continues to yield dividends to this day.

When people bring up ideas or needs to you as a leader, don't let your mind jump immediately to what you can do to provide a fix. First, think about whether this is something the community can or should do for themselves. Bring the issue to the church; then step back and see what happens. You may just be surprised to get something better than anything you personally could have come up with.

Quit Looking for Leaders and Start Building Them

Bob

Part of my dream of planting a multiplying church included the hope that everyone who was willing and able would be able to move quickly into exercising leadership. The reality was I kept waiting for leaders, but not many were stepping up. There weren't as many people ready for leadership as I had thought or hoped.

In more traditional churches, the practice is often to see a need, create a position and hire someone (usually from outside the community) to fill it. I knew that wouldn't—and with our limited resources, couldn't—be the way we did it. Eventually I realized that, for the most part, the way forward for us, and other churches like us, was to quit looking for leaders and start building them.

It starts with drawing a picture, casting vision for those in whom you see potential. Telling someone that in three years you'd like to see him or her become a key leader in our church or a potential elder has a wonderful effect on people. Those who pick up that vision, and desire what it is you are describing to them, often begin moving in that direction after they have it sketched out for them. It's almost as though the act of inviting them to consider it and move toward it begins to draw the leadership out of them, turning potential into actuality.

But what are we looking for in potential leaders? First, we're looking for people who are both able and willing to lead, because both are necessary. More specifically, we assess potential leaders based on five *Cs*: *character* (can they be trusted?), *competency* (do they have the specific skills necessary for the task or could they grow into those skills?), *chemistry* (how well do they connect and interact with others, and what impact would that have on others?), *calling* (is this something we—and they—would feel called to do, or is it simply just a good idea?) and *capacity* (are they the type of people that others currently follow or would want to follow)?

In addition to evaluation, we need to see and help them see the things that are standing in the way. Whether that may be elements of their character, or a lack of theological depth, it's our job as leaders to multiply ourselves and begin helping those who desire to grow into leadership to address whatever is keeping them from it.

Another important step is to allow other leaders to contribute to the search for and development of leaders. They may be able to help you as you equip someone either by providing valuable insight or by pointing out an area of concern that you have missed. More, they may see someone who would really benefit from your working with them that you otherwise might have overlooked. Developing leaders is a team project and should be approached in that way.

We've noticed that women who desire to be in leadership, especially those raised in evangelical circles, often have to be invited into it repeatedly. They have been told in subtle—and not so subtle—ways for years that certain church leadership roles are not open to them. It may come as no surprise that the women of your church are some of the most gifted, caring and wise leaders you could hope for. You may just need to be more proactive and purposeful in challenging potential leaders and inviting them to step into leading others. Conversely, you may have some that are ready and willing immediately and just need the leadership of the church to affirm them and desire to see them lead. For many, it's not enough to have a statement affirming women in leadership on our website; we have to work proactively to welcome, invite, encourage and affirm them in their leadership.

We committed years ago not to hire from outside our community. We felt it was a way of putting our money where our mouths were: if through discipleship and equipping community members we couldn't build the leaders we needed, we probably didn't deserve them.

Pay Your Taxes

Bob

This mantra actually has nothing to do with fiscal responsibility, but everything to do with the responsibility of leaders to allow others to discover, grow in, and hone their gifts within your community.

The way I learned to preach was by *doing it.* You learn to lead small groups by watching others do it and then doing it yourself. You learn to lead others in worship by watching others do it and then doing it yourself. And you learn to teach the community, to walk through passages of Scripture, teasing out what God was saying to them and what he's saying to us, by watching others do it and then doing it yourself. And really, that's the only way. Preaching classes may help, and may in fact be necessary, but it's real-world experience that turns aspiring worship leaders into actual ones, and hopeful teachers and preachers into those who can help lead a community through the Word of God.

I've come to view this process of helping others learn and grow in their gifts as a community tax that we all pay together. We know it's always a little difficult to listen to the first- or second-time preacher with all his or her trepidation and well-developed outline but not so well-developed delivery. I get nervous when we have a first-time preacher in our pulpit, or a first-time worship leader, because I know we'll have visitors present that Sunday, and I wonder what they'll think and feel about the less-than-confident or polished sermon or music we are being led by. But the community that pays the tax of, for instance, listening to a slightly less coherent message, or one with a less-than-Rob-Bell-mind-blow factor, or to a message that's slightly less entertaining or engaging than their usual preachers is making *an investment.*

The community invests in the new teacher they are being taught by. By engaging, listening and giving good feedback (both encouraging and constructive), they help that community member they love and who loves them and is doing his or her best to explore God's Word with them to learn how to do it better and better.

And the leader who knows what he or she is doing pays the tax by giving up his or her spot and making way for others. It's hard, especially in a series you feel passionate about, to let someone who hasn't done much, or any, preaching beyond a homiletics class take a week. But we do so joyfully, knowing this is how the body works. We make room. We defer to others. We lift others up and let them try and grow in their gifts.

To me, churches that don't do this but allow only skilled people to fill the pulpit or the worship leader's spot are shortsighted at best and miserly at worst. You may get better results in the short run by preaching forty-nine or fifty weeks out of the year, but in the long run, it's the community that suffers. Holding those places only for the best and brightest ensures that those who are beginners will have to go elsewhere to get the experience they need and desire. In other words, some community will pay the tax of allowing those nascent leaders to learn and grow—if not yours, then someone else's.

The reason I call it a tax is that I know there's a cost to the community. I've sat through enough seminarians' first-time sermons or first-time worship leaders to know it. People may not engage as much. Visitors may scratch their heads. But time and again, I've seen our regulars, who know the novices well, participate in spite of the lack of polish, cheering them on, helping them to learn. The regulars do it because of love, and because they intuit that the tax is not too high to pay to see someone flower in his or her gifts.

And sure, we've occasionally given people a chance and discovered together that no, that's not their gift—all part of paying taxes.

Is your community ready to count the cost of helping new leaders find their way? Invest in others. Pay the tax.

SECTION SEVEN

Opportunities

Just Jiggle the Doorknob

J.R.

The seven deadly words of the church: *we've never done it that way before.*

Churches can spend an exorbitant amount of time focusing on preserving the past when God desires for us to ask, "What might God have in store for us as we move forward?" In Acts we see the early church trying to hang onto the coattails of the Spirit, breathlessly attempting to keep up with where and how the Spirit is working. Acts is like a series of kingdom experiments rooted in love, faith and obedience guided by the work of the Spirit. These pioneers had a palpable anticipation that God was on the move.

Since the beginning of our church we've tried to cultivate a spirit of experimentation. In all wisdom and faith, we've attempted to follow the adventurous Holy Spirit into new places, new frontiers and new expressions. Some initiatives have been audacious, requiring large amounts of time, money and an ever-deepening prayer life. Others have been small and relatively simple initiatives. But all required risk, faith and courage.

We call these new initiatives "kingdom experiments." We use the language of experiment purposefully, as many experiments fail. Nobody expects all experiments to work (that's why they are called experiments). If these kingdom experiments fail, we assure our church, it's okay. And if they fail, let's learn from the experience and try something else.

We want to be a church that's willing to jiggle on the doorknob and see if the door is unlocked. If the door is locked, we can move on, attempting to discern where God may have us in other spaces.

But if it's unlocked, then, in faith, we open it and see what's behind the door. Part of jiggling on doorknobs is helping to cultivate a culture of experimentation, adaptability, risk and permission—even permission to fail. I've told our church that I'd rather we try something for the sake of the kingdom and fail than to have played it safe and never to have tried at all.

If we can create a culture that constantly seeks to stoke the coals of kingdom imagination in people by just jiggling on doorknobs, we might be surprised where and how God shows himself to us in the process. It doesn't mean we pursue every idea that comes our way. It doesn't mean we host and lead dozens of new church events each year. That would be both exhausting and unwise. However, jiggling on some doorknobs does mean that we can think creatively and courageously about how we might live our lives as followers of Christ and agents of the kingdom.

By casting a vision for these experiments we start, we hear people start conversations with phrases such as these:

- "Imagine if we . . ."
- "I wonder if God might be calling us to try . . ."
- "This may seem different, even a bit risky, but what if we pursued God by . . . ?"
- "Just think if we attempted to bless them by . . ."
- "What if God wants us to . . . ?"
- "What if we could try . . . ?"

These are the types of sentences that make us smile because they show us that people are willing to reach for the doorknob.

As we pray, dream, plan and process these experiments, we say, "Let's jiggle on the doorknob and see if it's unlocked. Let's see what happens." We believe that if God has provided for such a vision, he will unlock the appropriate doors. We don't believe breaking down a locked door is a way to move forward. That's spiritual manipulation. We also don't sit back passively and expect God to fling the door open every time either. That's passive and unengaged faith. We have a part to play, to jiggle on the handle and see if it's unlocked.

Don't simply assume the door of possibility is locked. Jiggle on it, and see what happens. If it's locked, we can trust God's sovereign purposes. But if it's unlocked, see it as a faith-filled opportunity and walk through, looking for what God may have in store.

If You Want to See God, Look for Red Jeeps

J.R.

I was fortunate enough to own my dream car in my twenties. It wasn't fancy. For months we saw a "for sale" sign in the window of a used, fire-engine-red Jeep Cherokee sitting in the driveway of the house about three blocks from where we lived. Several weeks later, with some keen negotiating skills, I was the proud owner of my dream. She was perfect. I was thrilled.

But it didn't take long for the thrill to wear off. The next day I was disappointed—even annoyed. Everywhere I looked—every intersection I stopped at, every parking lot I pulled into, every drive-through line—had a red Jeep Cherokee. They were *everywhere* (granted, we were living in Colorado at the time). However, it seemed that everyone had gone out and bought a red Jeep Cherokee. Of course, the truth is they'd been on the road all along; it was now that I began to notice them everywhere.

God drives a red Jeep Cherokee (at least that's what I'd like to believe anyway). If my eyes and heart are tuned to see him, I can recognize his presence in the world.

- God is in the smile of the little child at the park.
- He is in the interruption in my day by a friend who is hurting and in need of a listening ear.
- He's in the small interaction with the lady behind me in line at the post office.
- He's with me when I'm stuck in traffic.

- And he's with me on Sunday mornings in our church.

Rabbi Lawrence Kushner, in his unique interpretation of the account of the burning bush in Exodus 3, saw the story less as a dramatic miracle and more as a test God had for Moses. He writes:

> God wanted to find out whether or not Moses could pay attention to something for more than a few minutes. When Moses did, God spoke. *The trick is to pay attention to what is going on around you long enough to behold the miracle without falling asleep.* There is another world, right here within this one, whenever we pay attention.[1]

Can we see the miracle in the midst of the mundane without dozing off or getting bored and moving to the next thing? We look for God on Sundays and in the sensational, but can we see him at work Monday through Saturday in the subtle as well?

God is riding around in his jeep just waiting for us to spot him. Hidden in plain sight—isn't that just like God? The poet Elizabeth Barrett Browning, near the end of her piece *Aurora Leigh*, wrote these powerful lines:

> Earth's crammed with heaven,
> And every common bush afire with God;
> But only he who sees, takes off his shoes,
> The rest sit around it and pluck blackberries.[2]

God is often hidden in plain sight.

I've heard it countless times: Christians praying that God would be with us. But God has already promised his presence—he *is* with us. He promised that he would never leave us. His name is *Emmanuel.* Instead, we should pray for an *awareness of his presence in our lives* and thus the courage to respond faithfully.

What if our morning prayers sounded more like this?

God,
Surprise me today.
Give me sensitivity to see you at work.
Allow me to see you driving around in a red Jeep Cherokee throughout my day today.
Today I refuse simply to pick blackberries.
Amen.

In Your City There Is but One Church

J.R.

I was either foolish or naïve—or both. A few years ago I volunteered to direct our local gathering of pastors within our region. With no compelling vision, energy, focus, momentum or clear purpose behind it, it was floundering. Nobody was surprised. When I assumed the role, I thought long and hard about how to articulate a compelling and unifying kingdom vision of what could happen if we all worked together for the sake of God's kingdom in our region.

For several weeks prior to our launch, I invited pastors and key community leaders in our region to gather for a morning to talk about what a repurposed collection of pastors could look like—what we would call the North Penn Partnership of Churches. The room was full of several dozen pastors and leaders from various backgrounds and denominations—Episcopalians, Mennonites, Methodists, Baptists, Lutherans, Presbyterians, nondenominational churches and others. I sensed that if we focused on our differences, this initiative would quickly become divisive, lose momentum and suffer a slow but certain death. But if we were capable of latching onto a compelling vision—a vision larger than our individual churches—we might move forward with focus in where we were in agreement among other brothers and sisters in Christ.

As I began the meeting, I asked the room, "How many churches are in our region?" Some guessed fifty, others seventy, still others a hundred. I let the silence hang in the air for a moment and then said slowly, "The answer is one. In our city there is but *one church*." I reminded them that the kingdom of God is way bigger than each of our individual churches (and thank God for that). Different churches are different parts of the body and play different roles—and we need them all.

Our competition was not against the church down the street, but against the Evil One and his schemes: deception, death, abuse, hopelessness, self-centeredness, violence, fear, addictions and death. If we see one another as the competition, the Evil One rejoices; but if we see one another as teammates with different charisms working with the Spirit, then God's kingdom is evidenced much more clearly.

Our partnership of churches meets together monthly to pray, receive training, and update one another on significant events, issues and needs in our region. We also serve side-by-side once a year in a "community-service blitz" Saturday each spring. Pastors who've been in our community for twenty years and never met before are now getting together on occasion for lunch or coffee to listen, share stories and pray together. When a tragedy struck our community a few years ago, we came together to serve as a unified group. We often remind one another, "In our city there is but one church."

The kingdom of God is way bigger than your individual church. Too many churches I know believe their church is God's gift to the world. That's half right. The problem is most of those churches believe that *their* way of church is the *only* expression that honors God, and everyone else "just doesn't get it." As one church, our role then is to harness the power of partnerships for good kingdom mischief.

Jesus prayed for unity among the church and saw it as a way for the Father to receive more glory (see John 17). When the apostle Paul wrote to different churches throughout Asia Minor, he always addressed his letter "to the church in . . ." It was always singular. In his letter to the church in Ephesus, Paul describes how God gives different gifts to different people in the body (see Ephesians 4:11-13). But before mentioning differences, he stresses the crucial calling of unity among churches.

> Be completely humble and gentle; be patient, bearing with one another in love. Make every effort to keep the unity of the Spirit through the bond of peace. There is one body and one Spirit, just as you were called to one hope when you were called; one Lord, one faith, one baptism; one God and Father of all, who is over all and through all and in all. (Ephesians 4:2-6)

Body. Spirit. Hope. Lord. Faith. Baptism. God and Father of all. Paul wants us to know: there is but one church.

SECTION EIGHT

Success

Count What Matters

Bob

I knew we were in trouble the moment I realized it: most of what we talked about, most of what we were measuring during our staff and elder meetings, was attendance and offering. Additionally, we were failing to measure and count things such as how many people were being taught to be disciples in any intentional way, how many were connecting into home communities (or some other significant form of community in our church), and how many were responding to calls to pray and serve. I felt ashamed.

When we first started, as so many do, we were determined to do things differently than some of the larger or more traditional churches we had come from, where it seemed as though the emphasis was mainly on budgets and butts (in the pews). But it didn't take long before I was tracking attendance and giving on a spreadsheet, poring over the numbers carefully, wondering how we could make gains in both.

I've since made a conscious effort to decouple my emotions from both of those indicators. Sure, I still see reports in the weekly email to the community of what the giving is so far this month, but I try hard not to care too much about it, and rather to let our finances rest in God's hands and in the hands of the people in our community who have volunteered to give attention to them. I no longer track attendance numbers, preferring instead to give our people list a look each week, trying to remember who was there, and who hasn't been for a while, so I can reach out to those who have been missing.

More importantly, I've made a concerted effort in my heart and mind to care most about the biggest question of all: "How are we doing at making disciples?" After all, when Jesus left us, he didn't say, "Draw a big crowd." He said, "Make disciples." And so for us, that ought to be the most important indicator that our church is on the right track and therefore the thing we count. We should count how many people are being moved to serve others in some way, how many are connecting with others in community, and how many are taking up the challenge to learn more about the God we love and serve and how to live in the Way of Jesus.

Viewed in this light, how many people show up on a Sunday is about the least important thing we can count, and least likely to tell us how we are maturing as a community. This doesn't mean that being present for worship, the Lord's Table and the preaching of the gospel is unimportant—it's vitally important. It's simply that attendance there, divorced from other indicators, says little about the growth of an individual or a community.

Stop counting what matters little, and instead start counting what matters most—and help your church to know the difference.

Care More About Sending Capacity Than Seating Capacity

J.R.

A common question: "How many people were there on Sunday?" The more important question: "How are we equipping and unleashing people—through the love of the Father, through the power of the Spirit and in the name of the Son—to be faithful witnesses to Christ all the days of a week?"

This mantra, which we've used frequently since we first heard it from Rick Warren, is one of the most repeated mantras in the life of our church family. It brings into focus our calling: to equip, develop, unleash and release people into the world as salt and light. It is deeply significant when the church, the body of Christ, gathers together on Sunday mornings to worship the risen Christ. But the primary purpose of our local churches is not to fill the seats one day a week, but to fulfill the Great Commission (see Matthew 28:18-20). The role of pastors and elders is to develop more than recruit. We need to be about equipping, not entertaining—and we must focus our energies on unleashing authority, not merely delegating responsibility (see John 20:21).

Churches need to operate like airports.[1] Imagine you are waiting at the gate for your flight and you turn to the person next to you and ask, "So, are you going home or leaving home?" If the person responds by saying, "Oh, I'm not flying anywhere. I just come in everyday, watch people, hang out and then drive home," the response would certainly strike you as a bit odd. (In fact, you may be quick to relay that information to the nearest TSA agent.)

Why? Because that's not what airports are for. Airports exist to help people make their connections in order to go where they need to go. No one simply hangs out at airports. You don't go there to stay there—*you go there to go somewhere else.* Similarly, the role of the church is first to help people identify where they are being sent, and then help them faithfully make the connection to get there.

All of us matter in the kingdom. And all of us have a part to play in God's mission. When churches care more about their sending capacity than their seating capacity, it shifts the emphasis away from filling a building and toward filling the world with followers of Christ seeking to be salt and light in their particular contexts.

We know of a few churches that embrace this missionary posture in their new members' covenants. After going through a purposeful process of discernment and discipleship, each new member must identify his or her mission field. They share that mission field in front of the entire congregation—the hair salon or the insurance agency or the restaurant, the street they live on or the college campus where they study. The elders and leaders commission them and pray specifically for their mission fields. These churches act as airports in the kingdom of God.

All elements of a Sunday service are formative, but which element is the most significant? Well, it depends who you ask. Our brothers and sisters from a liturgical or high-church tradition might say the Eucharist. Those from a more charismatic background might say the times of worship and intercessory prayer. Those from a more evangelical or Bible-church background would say the sermon. (My guess is the Baptists would say the potluck in the fellowship hall following the service.) Mission-oriented churches might suggest the benediction. The benediction (from the Latin words *bene* and *dictus* meaning "the good word" or "the good saying") is a mix of blessing, challenge, reminder and charge. *We've gathered, been blessed and received. Now, let us scatter, bless and give to the world.*

Prioritizing sending capacity over seating capacity isn't a small tweak or a new paint job; it doesn't entail a few programmatic changes to the church calendar. No, it means cultivating a new ethos, shifting the paradigm and changing the posture of the community, which ultimately shapes everything the church is and does (as well as what it refuses to do). It's a perspective that is reflected in how the community thinks through being a church on mission. This has implications in church structure, staffing needs, the budget, leadership development and sermon series. It's not a checklist of what a church does; it's a change of DNA in how a church thinks about its role in the world. It's much more difficult, but infinitely more worthwhile.

Slay the Beast of Ambition Before It Slays You

J.R.

As a type-A oldest child and driven leader, I find that my RPMs are in the red zone much of the time. Sometimes this can be beneficial, but when left unchecked it can be incredibly detrimental to my soul—and also the souls of those I am called to lead.

I've had to repeat this phrase to myself and many other ministry leaders I've connected with. Ambition isn't inherently a bad thing. Drive and motivation can be helpful. Paul was quite an ambitious leader. Paul was careful to qualify his instruction to the Philippian church by telling them to do nothing out of *selfish* ambition (see Philippians 2:3).

Ambitious leaders attract other ambitious leaders. Sadly, my identity as a male in a North American context is determined way too easily by what I do and how well I do it. This runs counter to my gospel identity that tells me that, because of God's immense grace, I am not defined by what I do or how well I do it; I am defined by who I am and, most importantly, to whom I belong. Dallas Willard once said, "It turns out that what you really think about Jesus is revealed by what you do after you find out that you don't have to do anything."[1] Read that last sentence again slowly. It gets to the heart of motivation and ambition.

So, how do we slay the beast? It starts in the form of a question: "What's my motive?" Without proactive, careful, direct and frequent attention, ambition can add fuel to a dangerous fire. "What's driving me? Why? What's behind all of this ambition?" If I can get to the root of my motivations, I can, by God's grace, eliminate the detrimental effects of cancerous selfish ambition. This oftentimes-painful process leads to a much-needed realignment.

In my own life, the most ridiculously practical discipline that helps slay the beast is to practice sabbath religiously. Many pastors tell me they just can't bring themselves to do it. *I'm too busy. I have too much going on. People will think I am lazy. I wouldn't be able to think straight if I were just sitting around doing nothing for an entire day. I fear that the lack of progress and attention to my church will lead to its demise.*

All of these answers reveal to me even more how much they need to practice Sabbath. I've practiced Sabbath since the beginning of my pastoral calling, and admittedly, it hasn't been easy. Embarrassingly, it's oftentimes the most difficult day of my week to trust God. Deep down, some weeks I actually believe that our church will fall apart or that people truly *need* me today—or worse, that God needs me to keep the church together.

We often forget that Sabbath participation is one of the Ten Commandments. At times when I'm asked to speak on the topic, I title my talk "Nine Commandments and One Suggestion." Speaking of the "ten big ones," our friend A. J. Swoboda said, "If I have an affair, as a pastor I lose my job. But when I don't Sabbath, I get a raise." Our values are screwed up, and our theology is revealed in our schedules.[2]

It requires a lot of work to rest. There was a distinct moment on a restless Sabbath Monday that revealed my deep-seated self-reliance. I had justified to myself that I needed to check my voicemail messages and respond to emails. The Spirit whispered to me, "You think the church will fall apart? I made the entire universe and called you to this church. You may be the pastor of the church, but I am the head of the church. Trust me by resting." We must embed shalom into our schedules. Rest. Sleep. Trust.

Ruthlessly eliminating comparison from my life helps slay the beast, too. Not only does comparison rob me of joy, drain me of gratitude and fuel my insecurities, it tells me to push the gas pedal to do more, lead more, serve more and accomplish more.

Asking regularly what my motivation is, religiously practicing Sabbath and ruthlessly eliminating comparison out of my life help to address my racehorse tendencies and slay the ambition beast.

God longs to put to death our ministry ambitions in order to resurrect intimacy with him.

Slay the beast before it slays you.

It's Kingdom, Not Competition

Bob

When we first decided to plant a church in 2003, I did what many aspiring church planters do: I called and emailed as many other pastors and church planters as I could in an effort to sit down with them, introduce myself and learn from them. I expected a warm welcome to the club, words of encouragement, prayers and heartfelt offers of help. I received some encouragement, but the majority of what I got was suspicion and discouragement. I was shocked. It was disheartening to be seen as a competitor when my desire was to link arms in partnership. I learned that not everyone sees a new church as a sign that God is at work.

A few years after we planted, I began to receive those same calls and emails from other church planters. I then understood what those pastors I had contacted felt. I knew I needed to begin guarding my heart. I knew what it was like to be seen as the competition. Now on the other side, I never wanted to feel that way toward other pastors, even though that was the inclination of my own heart.

I began to repeat to myself, "It's kingdom, not competition." When I heard of a new church, I said it to myself and prayed for them. When I read an article about an innovative ministry initiative that was met with great results, I repeated the mantra to myself; I would pause and thank God for what he was doing in that local church. I repeated it to our church on those occasions when we prayed for other communities together. And hardest of all, I continue to say it to myself when people leave our church to attend another one.

Praying for other church communities, celebrating their successes and doing everything we can to partner with, support and cheer on what they are doing in our city has formed in our leadership and in our community a beautiful, unifying kingdom spirit.

Sadly, I know of one church that kept a list of "competitors." All the churches in the surrounding area and what they were doing were on the list, regularly updated so the leadership would know what the "competition" was up to. I can honestly say I have yet to come across a more dysfunctional church, and I believe their "competitor's list" and the heart behind it were a big part of what was behind the dysfunction.

Tell your church often about what God is doing elsewhere. Help them to cheer on what is happening in and being done by other communities. Pray for other communities, and welcome them into your neighborhood or city with open arms and hearts. Continually tell yourself and everyone in your church: "It's kingdom, not competition."

Whatever Is Happening Now Will Not Keep Happening Forever

Bob

One of the main tricks in life, I believe, is not to extrapolate current conditions and circumstances off into the future. However, that's exactly the tendency we have as humans, and especially, I've discovered, as ministry leaders. We look at things now and think they will always be that way.

We long to see landmarks in the road, mileposts that tell us either we have now reached the pinnacle, the place we always dreamed of being (even if that place is only "stability"), or conversely, that the bottom has fallen out and now is the time to bail. But the mileposts are merely markers on the journey, telling us where we are now, promising nothing of the journey ahead.

And so, when things are good, we see nothing but success and good times stretching out in front of us. In the depths of despair, during the most challenging times of life and ministry, we feel as though the darkness has become the new normal. The reality is much more complex: there are always better times ahead, and worse ones as well.

During those dark times, when ministry becomes more of a weight than a joy, I tell myself, "Whatever is happening now will not keep happening forever." Those words have kept me through relational breaks in our staff that seemed unfixable, through budget woes when we didn't think we were going to meet payroll, through even a time when our community lost a third of its members because we had let a beloved pastor go. In this way I have found hope.

In the same way, during the successful times when we were growing, budget was bigger than ever and new people were engaging with the church seemingly every week, I continued to tell myself, "What is happening now will not keep happening forever." In this way I have found a measure of humility.

There's another way to read this mantra as well, one that encourages us not to miss what is happening *right now* as we overly focus on where we'd like to be or what we'd like to see happen.

The challenge of ministry, like the challenge of life in general, is to be present to what's happening *now*. Too many single people miss the joys of singleness by longing to be married. Too many young married couples miss the joys of the early years without children because they long to be parents. Too many parents of young children miss the joys of the infant years, longing for the days when their children are more independent, less dependent on them for everything. And on it goes.

In the same way we in ministry can miss the joys of a small, close community by looking at larger communities and wishing we had their resources and influence. We can miss the inherent learning and even joy of being shoulder to shoulder in community with others through challenging times because the difficulties and pain we are experiencing mask the ways in which we are being brought together, the ways in which we are being formed and the invaluable things we are learning.

In life, and in ministry, remember: how it is now is not how it will always be. Learn to appreciate how things are now, but also take comfort in the fact that if things are difficult, there are better days ahead. Stay humble because no success is forever. Stay hopeful because, in Christ, no failure is permanent.

SECTION NINE

Self-Management, Spirituality and Personal Issues

Enjoy the Front-Row Seat

Bob

As a pastor, I get to see things that most people don't. I regularly stand two feet from men and women as they pledge their lives and their love to one another with tears streaming down their faces. I am, quite literally, the only person in the room who can see the faces of the bride and the groom and all their family and friends at once—all the joy, all the anxiety, all mixed together in one blessed moment.

It's amazing. The pressure I used to feel that I would mess things up (after all, who wants to be *that* pastor—the one who calls the bride by the wrong name or accidentally skips the vows) has now given way simply to feeling honored at being invited so close to something so intimate.

In fact, that's how I've come to answer most every request I get to perform a wedding: "I'd be honored." And I mean it. That's how I've come to feel about dealing with some of the harder stuff, too.

The first few times I had to sit with a couple who was in crisis, I hated it. I hated feeling (inaccurately, I should add) that the weight of their marriage and family was resting on my shoulders, feeling as though if I said the wrong thing, or failed to say the right thing, their marriage would dissolve and I'd be to blame.

But one time, as I sat with a couple processing an infidelity, I found myself almost smiling. Not because anything was funny, because at that point, little was. No, I was smiling inwardly because once more I was in the front row. This couple had honored me with a seat at their deepest pain, trusting me to be a faithful presence who would hold up the hope God brings us in Christ during one of the darkest hours of their lives. It felt no less a privilege than standing before a couple exchanging vows.

I felt the same way the first time I sat with a couple that had lost a child, in preparation for her funeral. What a heart-wrenching, tragic situation to walk into. What a privilege to bring good news into the midst of despair.

Don't get me wrong, though; I still don't relish the hard issues—the confrontations, the hospital visits in dire sickness, the marriages that are falling apart. I have just come to realize that if I fight involvement in those things internally, I will "mess it up." I'll be less present than I need to be. I'll look for easy ways out. I'll do my "job" and move on—and that, frankly, is a poor way to approach something as sacred as the entrée we're given into the hardest parts of people's lives.

It's better to lean in, to feel honored to sit with people in their sickness or in their moment of grief. It's better to feel the weight of being trusted by God to be present at the birth of a piece of someone's character that is forged in grief or in confrontation and (hopefully) resolution.

Too often we look at some of these life moments as the least desirable parts of pastoral ministry, the parts that take the most from us. To enjoy the front-row seat is to feel the privilege we have to be ministers of the gospel in the marriages, and all the joy they bring. It's to feel that privilege in the midst of the arguments and the strife, too, as well as in the forgiveness, the growth and the healing that God can and does work in those situations.

Let Your Calendar Say No

Bob

Ministry seems to oscillate between being busy and being insanely busy. One of the most difficult tasks a ministry leader faces is managing his or her time—which ultimately means we must learn how to say no.

We were just starting our church, things were busy and I had not yet established good rhythms of when I would do which pieces of my work. People would call and ask for an appointment, and I would make one with them at whatever time was most convenient for them. At times I was having two or three appointments a day, not to mention other scheduled meetings with staff and elders.

The problem came when I realized I was struggling to fit in all those things I needed to do that had no set time in my schedule—things like working on a sermon, sending out the weekly email, putting together the worship order and making sure we had people to do all the things we were going to do that week. Every appointment I made pushed those things farther and farther into the week until I frequently found myself working on my weekend days off just to catch up.

The solution was common sense, and common sense came in the form of a book by Eugene Peterson, *The Contemplative Pastor*:

> When I appeal to my appointment calendar, I am beyond criticism. If someone approaches me and asks me to pronounce the invocation at an event and I say, "I don't think I should do that; I was planning to use that time to pray," the response will be, "Well, I'm sure you can find another

> time to do that." But if I say, "My appointment calendar will not permit it," no further questions are asked. If someone asks me to attend a committee meeting and I say, "I was thinking of taking my wife out to dinner that night; I haven't listened to her carefully for several days," the response will be, "But you are very much needed at this meeting; couldn't you arrange another evening with your wife?" But if I say, "The appointment calendar will not permit it," there is no further discussion. The trick, of course, is to get to the calendar before anyone else does. I mark out the times for prayer, for reading, for leisure, for the silence and solitude out of which creative work—prayer, preaching, and listening—can issue.[1]

As I began to put Peterson's wisdom into practice, time began to feel a bit more manageable, and ministry a bit less rushed and hectic. Blocking out time for preparation, for study, for planning and for praying first, and saying, "Sorry, I have something on the calendar for that time," when someone asked for an appointment during one of those hours, allowed me to get done what I needed to get done, and put the appointments in the other, free and empty spaces. When I looked at my calendar and saw "sermon prep," I had good reason not to answer the phone or check email.

The truth is, I hate saying no to people. You probably do, too. After all, we got into ministry to be involved in significant work in the lives of people we care about. But thoughtless and undiscerned yeses, separated from the context of our day or week, lead to diminished effectiveness. We rush frenetically from one appointment to another, hoping all the while we'll be able to catch up later.

Will Willimon, in his book *Pastor*, quotes Stanley Hauerwas as describing most pastors as "quivering masses of availability."

Willimon continues, "Practicing what I call 'promiscuous ministry'—ministry with no internal, critical judgment about what care is worth giving—we become victims of a culture of insatiable need."[2]

Let your calendar say no for you.

Keep the Gumball Machine Full

J.R.

Less than two years into full-time ministry, I was on the fast track to burnout. Fortunately, my supervisor recognized the situation and intervened, forcing me to take time off in order to rest. I visited a counselor for the first time in my life, sharing how overwhelmed, exhausted and depleted I felt. I was sprinting the marathon and falling apart. As Dan sat listening to me, he began doodling on a yellow legal pad. I was confused, wondering if he was bored.

After a few awkward moments of drawing, Dan tore off the paper and handed it to me. "It's a gumball machine," he said. *Actually, it's a very poorly drawn picture of a gumball machine,* I thought. I was skeptical and a bit annoyed. *I paid a hundred dollars to tell a guy my story, and he draws me a bad picture of a gumball machine—are you serious?* But he explained: "Right now your gumball machine is empty. There's nothing left. We've got to figure out how we get it refilled. We either lessen the outflow of gumballs, increase the inflow of gumballs or both. Those are the options if you're going to last in ministry."

He said I needed to put an "Out of Order" sign on my life right now. "It's time to unscrew the lid of the gumball machine and ask the Holy Spirit to refill it with more gumballs."

This made sense. It not only showed me the significance of rest and replenishment, but it offered me hope to live into healthier ministry rhythms for the long haul.

Dan prayed for me, and I left. As I walked to my car, I realized I had the best hundred-dollar picture of a gumball machine I could ever own. I placed Dan's drawing above my desk; every time I looked at it I'd ask: "How are my gumballs? Is my gumball machine low? If so, how can we refill the gumballs?"

While I can't control the chaos and crises of ministry, what I can control is entering into healthy rhythms and making sure I take care of myself so that I can serve others.

Over the years I've asked countless kingdom leaders: "So, how are your gumballs?" In fact, I began to ask that question of them so much that when I felt God call me out of a church in Colorado to serve at a church in Philadelphia, the leadership team gave me a gumball machine as a going-away gift. That gumball machine remains in the corner of my office as a frequent reminder: I cannot serve in ministry over the long haul with an empty gumball machine.

Authentic ministry derives from the overflow of our lives; and if we're empty, we have little to give to others. We may be able to fake it for a while, but ultimately an empty gumball machine will catch up to us. I remember being jolted to attention as I sat in a room full of pastors when James Bryan Smith told us, "Pastor, make caring for your soul your primary activity or get out of the ministry." He was talking about our gumball machines.

The World Needs More Well-Rested Leaders

J.R.

It's troubling how few leaders are well rested. When I speak about this with leaders, I ask them to name three well-rested ministry leaders. No one has ever given me an answer. Former US president Bill Clinton one said, "Every major mistake I've ever made in my life is due directly to the fact that I had little rest."[1] Maybe one of the most spiritual things we can do this week is take a nap.[2]

We live in a culture that values busyness and celebrates workaholism as if it were a badge of honor. Sadly, the church has not been immune to this cultural value system. As church leaders we perpetuate the problem. When was the last time you received the compliment, "You are such a rested leader. Thanks for caring for us by caring for your own body and soul by getting appropriate sleep"?

Admittedly, I am no expert in this area—which is why this mantra is so necessary in my own life. I have an unhealthy habit of staying up too late after my family has gone to bed. I'm not wasting my time with trivial things. In fact, oftentimes, I'm studying, responding to crucial emails, visiting someone in the hospital, reading a soul-shaping book, preparing for my next teaching—even writing and editing this book. The problem is that I go to bed exhausted and wake up in the morning feeling irritable, cranky, impatient and lacking joy. It's not that the things I was doing were bad; it's the fact that I was doing things when I should have been resting.

Judaism has a beautiful redemptive view of the Sabbath rest. Jews practice *Shabbat* from sundown Friday to sundown Saturday.

The reason? The rhythm comes right out of the creation account in Genesis 1. Each day of creation is marked off with the repeated phrase: "there was evening, and there was morning—the first day . . .," "there was evening, and there was morning—the second day . . .," and so on. Following the order of creation, Jews begin the day by making a faith statement: *the first thing they do each day is to do nothing at all.* They sleep.

Their faith began not with doing something, but with stopping everything to rest. And when one wakes up in the morning, it's a faith statement that God has already been at work in this day long before we began participating in it—an acknowledgment that this is God's world, not ours. As Charles Spurgeon said, "God gave us sleep to remind us we are not him." With this, we can work from rest, rather than rest from work. Therefore, being purposeful about rest isn't just a good idea; it's nonnegotiable.

In 1 Kings 19 God speaks to the prophet Elijah via a gentle whisper—or, as it has been famously translated, "a sound of sheer silence" (1 Kings 19:12 NRSV). But there is another crucial element in the story. In a chapter prior, Elijah participated in one of the most miraculous acts of any prophet in Israel atop Mount Carmel with the 450 prophets of Baal. But now he's running for his life. He's exhausted—and suicidal.

God restores him in three seemingly "unspiritual" ways: with food, drink and sleep. Elijah took a nap. Then, an angel of the Lord nudged him awake and told him to eat hot cakes and drink water provided for him. Food. Water. Sleep. Sacred gifts. The physical and the spiritual are much more connected than we realize. The care of our bodies affects our souls, just as the care of our souls affects our bodies.

What if a peaceful and well-rested presence was the clearest evidence of our trust in Christ? Instead of living with anxious work-aholism and identity-stealing exhaustion, what if God's people were faithfully, counterculturally communicating to the world that there is a better, more hope-filled way to live?

Well-rested leaders are on the endangered-species list. And when we model rest to our churches, they begin to see rest as a crucial spiritual discipline and a gift from God, not a necessary evil.

When we purposefully choose rest, we model what it means to receive grace from God. Choose rest before you are forced into it.

Soft Hearts, Thick Skin

Bob

To say that ministry can be hard is an understatement. It might be more accurate to say that ministry can be hardening. The impact of seemingly unending criticism, putting out relational fires and dealing with toes that have been stepped on can have a deadening effect on our hearts. If we're not careful, we begin to care less and less, and to feel ever less empathy for those who are going through hard times, or having a hard time with us.

On the other hand, the impact of all that criticism or relational discord can leave us not only hardhearted toward others, but also overly sensitive to our own feelings of being slighted, accused or questioned.

The mantra "soft hearts, thick skin" captures perfectly not only a very Jesus-like attitude toward others, but also a mindset critical to survival in ministry. I plucked this mantra from an offhand comment made by a fellow pastor and friend of ours, Mandy Smith. I can't even recall the specific context in which she said it, but it resonated deeply in my soul. Pastor and author Stuart Briscoe said something very similar: "Qualifications of a pastor [or any Christian leader]: the mind of a scholar, the heart of a child, and the hide of a rhinoceros."

Nobody had a softer heart toward others than Christ. The Gospels tell us over and over again how he was moved by compassion, moved to tears even, on behalf of others. And yet criticism, disdain and outright rejection seemed to roll off his back. None of those ever seemed to make him question his calling or mission. He may have had a soft heart, but he certainly had thick skin.

Recently, I've had plenty of opportunity to practice this mantra, and soon you will, too. Being misunderstood, offending people unintentionally, hurting feelings and stepping on toes are all a part of ministry because they are all a part of being human. The only unknown is what you will allow those things to work in you. Will they give you a hard heart and soft skin? An overconcern for your own standing, reputation and self-image? It's better to allow them to form in you a soft heart, open to the feelings and hurts of others, and a thick skin that makes you able to turn the other cheek, not paying back evil for evil and returning love and blessings for insult. The choice is one we make daily as we repeat to ourselves, "Soft heart, thick skin."

Learn the Unforced Rhythms of Grace

J.R.

Are you tired? Worn out? Burned out on religion? Come to me. Get away with me and you'll recover your life. I'll show you how to take a real rest. Walk with me and work with me—watch how I do it. Learn the unforced rhythms of grace. I won't lay anything heavy or ill-fitting on you. Keep company with me and you'll learn to live freely and lightly. (Matthew 11:28-30 *The Message*)

Few verses have I shared more with kingdom leaders out of Eugene Peterson's *The Message* translation than this one. Sadly, we've met too many pastors who try to serve and lead out of exhaustion and frenetic activity. It's all too rare to meet a ministry leader whose rhythms feel free, light and saturated with peace—who purposefully keep company with Christ in order to learn how to live this way.

Jesus invited his disciples into a way of life that was freely available to them. The great news is this is still available to us today. Jesus isn't giving pithy fortune-cookie sayings. He is offering us life at the highest and purest measure—to watch how he does it like a master would teach his apprentices. Each word in this passage is weighted with meaning, but the most striking phrase is "Learn the unforced rhythms of grace."

Learn: Life with Christ happens from a humble posture of learning, being fully convinced that Jesus has something significant to teach us if we'll let him. We see him not just as Savior and Lord, but also as the master teacher.

Unforced: In a world that seems to force itself upon us, dictating what we should and should not do, we are called into a life that is unforced. When the movement of life is unforced, it is beautiful to watch. Bring force into the mix, and it brings legalism, guilt and fear. If we've ever been to a middle school dance, we know what awkward and forced rhythms look like. They're difficult to watch. But we've also see the rhythms of a gifted dancer. Natural. Graceful. Unforced. Beautiful. Life with God is a dance. A life best lived is one in which we enter into rhythms that are unforced—rhythms that just *flow.*

Rhythms: Rhythms bring consistency and stability, but they are not ruts. They are practices saturated in life and liveliness. We are drawn to Jesus as he draws us into his rhythms of life. While rhythms anchor us, they can also bring texture, depth and spontaneity.

Grace: Grace, of course, is the fuel that the engine of the gospel runs on. Life-giving rhythms rooted in grace are incredibly beautiful and attractive. In fact, it is impossible to have forced rhythms of grace. *Grace is always unforced.* It's what makes it so amazing.

Learn the unforced rhythms of grace. And invite others into those rhythms with you, showing them that they're not only possible to learn, but also available.

The Only Thing You Should Be Anxious About Is Having a Nonanxious Presence

Bob

When Paul wrote that we ought not be anxious about anything, he was giving leaders better advice than perhaps most of us have ever realized. One of the dangers involved in leading a church is that we often find ourselves moving from crisis to crisis, solving one problem only to have to begin working on another.

Without proper self-management, the anxiety we tend to naturally feel at times of intense stress can morph from being acute—that is, a natural response to a real threat—into being chronic. Chronic anxiety is when our bodies and minds become unable to bounce back from the fight-or-flight hyperawareness that can actually be lifesaving in the midst of real danger. The same instincts that can save our lives or the lives of others in a moment of danger can become life-sapping and actually destroy our bodies when they lead to the kind of anxiety that produces sleeplessness, overworked adrenal glands, and a compromised immune system.

Leaders are less like thermometers and more like thermostats than we realize. Our level of calmness or anxiety has a significant impact on the church as a whole. People can tell when their leaders are stressed and they begin to take on that stress themselves, often without even realizing it. The anxiety moves through the whole system—from the leaders, to the staff around them, to the people they are ministering to. It's difficult to overstate the impact of an anxious leader on the community he or she is leading. His or her anxiety becomes the community's anxiety. Instead of responding in measured ways to problems, we begin reacting indiscriminately to crises. And to an anxious leader, and by extension to their community, everything becomes a crisis. The higher the level of chronic anxiety in a church community, the more difficult it is for it to respond correctly to one another, or to the normal stresses of life together.

The answer is to become a self-differentiated leader.[1] Self-differentiated leaders are those who know who they are apart from who they believe others think them to be. That is, their identity is secure whether things are going well or going poorly, and whether they feel as though others are approving of them or not in any given moment. Only self-differentiated leaders are able to lead with calmness, free from the anxiety that often causes us to make rash, hasty decisions of reactivity rather than prayerful, measured responses to the issues that will inevitably arise in ministry.

As I remind myself that my identity is secure in Christ, that in his kingdom I am always safe, and that whatever problem I may be looking at in the moment is temporary, I discover that one of the best gifts I can give my community is the gift of a nonanxious presence.

Part Two

MANTRAS FOR

THE COMMUNITY

SECTION ONE

Expectations

We Will Let You Down: If We're Close Enough to Help, We're Close Enough to Hurt

Bob

Nobody wants to be the church that hurts people. But at some point, every church ends up doing just that.

Early in our church life we came to the painful realization that as much as we were determined to be a church that healed and not hurt, human nature and our own sinful tendencies were going to make it impossible to never cause hurt to anyone. More, we discovered that the nature of community ensured that at some point, some hurt would happen.

As we moved through the early years of our church, we realized just how much emotional weight people were putting on the community. The fact that they had found in our church a safe place to be in process, a place where it seemed they could be their authentic selves and form close relationships, meant that when something happened that confused or consternated them, the dissonance between the idealized version of church that they held in their heads and hearts and the real flesh-and-blood community they were participating in felt like a betrayal.

That's when we knew we had to develop some language around the issue and help people to realize that at some point we, the pastors or other elders, or other people in the community, or perhaps the church as a whole, were going to let them down. We would not recognize or use their gifts in the ways they hoped we would. We would say something from the pulpit or make a decision as elders that they disagreed with or found hurtful. We would go left when everything in them screamed "right!"

We wanted people to do three things with that information. First, we wanted them to know in advance that it was coming, so that when it happened it wasn't a shock. It's not as though we were claiming to be a perfect community, and certainly no one has ever said that they thought we were. But forewarning people that we would eventually let them down in some way seemed to lessen the impact when it happened.[1]

Second, we really wanted people to understand that the cost of real community is vulnerability to hurt. We loved all the close relationships we were seeing as people moved in together into community houses, or formed new friendships through our church as they found people who had been on a similar journey. But the cost of being close to others is that they now have the ability to step on your toes—hard. The closer the relationship, in fact, the more potential it has for impact in our lives, both positive and negative. As we occasionally had to come in and help untangle some knots people had gotten into with one another, we reminded them that if we're close enough to help, we're close enough to hurt. The only way to ever ensure we will never be hurt in community is to keep people at a distance, but that means cutting ourselves off from all the ways those people could help us as well.

And third, we wanted people to comprehend the inevitable struggles of "life together" as a means that God uses in order to form us. The question wasn't whether or not we would disappoint them; it was what they would do with that disappointment when it happened. Would it drive them away from community, or would it deepen their commitment to see the life of Jesus worked out among us? Would it skew their view of God, or would it drive them into his arms? Would they learn to address the pain they were feeling as a result of others' words and actions, or would they remain silent, growing ever more bitter?

We use this mantra regularly to help people not only to have a realistic view of community, but also to have a formation view of what happens in community, especially some of the harder parts. As people come to your church, remind them of the potential costs and pains of community, and encourage them toward formation even through the letdowns, frustrations and disappointments that will surely occur.

Everything Is an Experiment

Bob

Our early days as a community were marked largely by an effort to answer the question, "Who are we going to be as a community?"

In answer to that question we established certain "core values" and out of those tried various activities, initiatives and ways of doing ministry. I probably don't need to tell you that not everything "worked." In fact, most things didn't.

In the middle of that, I began to notice a certain amount of whiplash among the community, as one way of trying to see something done in our community would give way to another and then again to yet another. People seemed confused—confused as to why we would change so easily while we were still trying to figure out who we would be. Every change felt a bit like a failure, and those failures were adding up.

I knew we'd need to address that and attempt to normalize trying new things and even failing at new things. In the minds of many in our community, every failure was another sign that things weren't working and that our community was on tenuous ground. In my mind, though, every failure was a step toward figuring out what would really work!

Worse, some things that "worked" when we were small worked increasingly less well as we grew. When we were thirty people, we were able to gather in someone's house for a monthly "community dinner." As we grew, that became increasingly less possible. But that was difficult for people to see.

We realized that unless we got a handle on this, we would end up stuck—stuck being a community that was either unwilling to risk and fail, or unwilling to change and let go of what used to work but no longer did. I really didn't want to be either.

It was at that point that we began to say frequently, "Everything is an experiment." I could feel the results immediately. Letting people know as we started something new that we were looking at it as a possibility that might work for our community rather than as a something we were committing to now and for all time allowed people to invest, see how things panned out and yet hold things with an open hand. In addition to saying, "Everything is an experiment" a lot, we've also put this mantra into tangible practice by putting time limits on things. We'll say, "Let's try this for nine months," or "We're going to try it this way this year." If it works, great. We can keep doing it. But if it doesn't, and we have to change direction, people are much less likely to feel as though the community as a whole has taken a step backward.

Saying, "Everything is an experiment" frequently creates a culture of experimentation. People are more willing to step out, try new initiatives and join in existing experiments when they know that there is little pressure to avoid failure.

Encourage your community to be experimental, to take risks and to see everything that doesn't work as just another step toward figuring out what does.

Go Sailing with God

J.R.

The first time I went sailing was on my Uncle Ray's sailboat in the Tampa Bay. During our outing he taught us all sorts of things: how to read the wind, how to take care of the rigging, how to notice the conditions out in the water and, ultimately, how to enjoy the process. It was a great deal of fun, but it was also exhausting—much more than I imagined. The situation changed quickly. Conditions altered in the matter of minutes. But when we were sailing at great speed across the bay, it was such a rush.

That day marked me deeply when I realized the similarities between sailing and living the *with-God* life. I had heard the sailing metaphor numerous times before, but had never actually experienced it firsthand. More than anything, my experience sailing was about *participating*, working together with others as we sought to work with forces that were stronger than ourselves. We all had a part to play, but we didn't have the only part to play. Sailing is nothing more than participation with people as we seek to work with wind and water.

Throughout the years, many Christians have told me they long for God to work in their lives. But they had a passive approach to how God would work in the world. They believed that their role was to sit back, curled up in the corner in the fetal position, and just wait for God to do his thing; and, if he wanted their involvement, he'd tap them on the shoulder and tell them. "God is all-powerful, and he is going to do whatever he wants to do," one gentleman told me. As spiritual as that may sound, he possessed a perspective that he was a victim to God's fate—for good or ill—and he had no role in the matter.

But throughout the years, I've also talked with Christians on the other end of the spectrum. They told me that they believed that it was their duty to "get the job done." They believed they were in the driver's seat, making decisions based on what they wanted. And, at the last moment, they'd invite God to bless the process. He was simply the hood ornament on the car of their lives.

That day in the Tampa Bay helped me see what it meant to participate with God in our everyday lives. We have a role to play—but ultimately God works as he desires. Sailing requires a dependence upon the conditions of the wind and the current of the water. It's similar to what Paul said to the church in Colossae: "I work and struggle so hard, depending on Christ's mighty power that works within me" (Colossians 1:29 NLT).

Without the wind, we would be stuck in the middle of the bay just floating along. Without the wind, sailing is impossible. But imagine if we put our boat out in the middle of the water, yet refused to learn the ropes, hoist the sails or read the movement of the wind. The wind might be blowing, but we would still just be floating in the middle of the bay.

I've seen sailboats with a 200 HP motor installed off the back. Sure, you can get across the other side of the lake with relative ease and comfort that way, *but that's not what a sailboat was made for.* Those who only use the motor on the back of their sailboats will never know the thrill, the rush and the joy that comes from truly sailing.

In many ways, spiritual disciplines are like learning the ropes in order to sail with God. These lessons aren't the same as the event of sailing itself, but they help to enable me so that when the conditions are right, sailing can occur as it was intended to be. But we are utterly aware that sailing is absolutely impossible if not for the presence of the wind moving through our sails, which keeps us grounded in humility and in deep dependence upon him.

We can't control the timing, direction or movement of the wind. But we can control how we read the conditions and how to position our boat in such a way as to harness the full power of the wind. As a seventeenth century French theologian wrote, "The wind of God is always blowing, but you must hoist your sail." Sailing with God can be a lot of work—but it's a thrill!

Learning Is Often Preceded by Unlearning

J.R.

Many people are educated well beyond their capacity for obedience. For those who have grown up in church, it can be easy to assume that learning is the sole way in which we grow as followers of Christ. Sadly, we have divorced orthopraxy from orthodoxy.

I've known Jesus for more than three decades. What I find so fascinating in this journey with Christ is that the more I encounter him, the more I need to unlearn. What I thought he wanted from me needs to be reimagined—constantly. What I believed about the kingdom of God needed—and, at times, still needs—to be reexamined. What I thought God felt about me needed—and, at times, still needs—realignment. I need to unlearn inaccurate perspectives, incomplete understandings and skewed values of life in the kingdom. My understandings of violence, power, identity, money, worry, the role of women in church leadership, national pride, poverty, prayer, relationships, race, the Holy Spirit and privilege (just to name a few) have had to go through a significant process of unlearning. In fact, they still do.

When Jesus arrives on the scene and begins his public ministry, he says, "The kingdom of heaven has come near [is here]. Repent and believe the good news!" (Mark 1:15). Repent—*metanoia*—can be translated as "to pull a U-turn." Jesus is saying, "Rethink your way of life and how you've viewed God's role in it." In other words, *unlearn*. Rethink. Reimagine. And once you've done that, start to learn rightly. *To unlearn is to repent. To learn is to believe.*

Each year our church launches a new cohort of what we call the Men's Discipleship Group, a group of guys committed to participate intensely in an apprenticeship in the Way of Jesus over several weeks. Many tell me at the end of the cohort that the ways they were shaped most significantly were not by what they learned, but by what they unlearned. This encourages me greatly.

The Gospels are a compilation of stories that could be titled "Adventures in Missing the Point." The disciples seem to believe they know what God is like. Jesus repeatedly has to correct their basic assumptions about God and the kingdom he is establishing. They are slow learners. On more than one occasion Jesus becomes impatient with their inaccurate views of the kingdom. They argue over who is the greatest when he tells them it's about serving and being the least. They brush kids away from Jesus—and then Jesus lays into them for doing such a thing. Jesus' parables are creative stories told to lop off some assumption about the nature of reality and to facilitate unlearning so that true learning can actually begin. Stories told effectively and questions asked skillfully are two of the most common and effective ways Jesus challenges assumptions and throws unlearning parties for his guests.

A common question we ask in our church is this: "Where do you need to experience unlearning in order to grasp an accurate picture of Jesus and life in the kingdom?" The kingdom is upside-down, backward and seemingly inside out, full of paradoxes and blindsiding truth (and then we often realize the truth has been right under our noses the entire time). Unlearning, learning and relearning—all these are necessary elements of life in the kingdom of God.

Unlearning is painful and humbling—sometimes humiliating. And yet some of the most long-lasting and fruitful growth I've seen in the people in our church has been when they were challenged to unlearn long-held assumptions about the reality of power, sexuality, violence, compassion, justice and the poor, to name a few.

Unlearning is crucial to the process of soul-forming discipleship.

Make Room for Questions and Doubt, but Don't Make a Value out of Not Knowing

Bob

One of the draws of our community at its inception was that it was a place where doubt and questions were okay. We sought to create a safe place for people to hear the wild message of Jesus. We knew this was important to the unchurched and formerly churched we were attempting to engage. We also knew from talking to others that many had left church because they felt that rock-solid certainty was too often expected, if not required. This certainty extended from the important stuff like "Who is Jesus?" and "What is the gospel?", all the way down to minor theological points. Conformity with how the leadership saw all of those things was expected. Many told us that being okay with people's struggles and doubts was a breath of fresh air.

But we began to notice a pattern over the years. We saw many come to our community, open about their doubts concerning God, Jesus, church and the Bible. And yet years later, they still had the same exact questions and doubts. Nothing had changed. Not wanting to cease being a place where doubt was okay, we began to modify our mantra when we talked about the kind of community we wanted to be, and added " . . . but don't make a value out of not knowing."

We really want to push people to take an active stance toward their doubts. We want them to wrestle with the questions that make faith hard for them, read books, talk to others in our community, including the pastors, and not rest until there's some resolution. Sure, some questions will never be answered, but no question should go unanswered for a simple lack of trying.

With the first part of this mantra we prepare the community for the skeptics and undecideds who will surely come, but who usually feel silenced. We normalize the doubt that many committed Christians in our midst still struggle with. And we throw the welcome mat out for those who may wonder if church can really be a safe place for them, even with all the baggage of doubt and confusion over Christianity they may be carrying.

With the second part we encourage people to doubt their doubts, seek answers and not be content not to know. If this Jesus story we tell is true, it's the absolute most important thing, not only in the world, but also in each individual life. And as such, it deserves concerted effort to figure out, to understand and to embrace.

Being a community for doubters and skeptics can be hard work. But conversely, a community where everyone already believes and no one wrestles with questions (at least that they will admit) leads me to believe that its value of mission has gone cold. A true missional community will be filled to the brim with people all over the place in their faith. Our job is to make room for them, their doubts and their questions, and appropriately challenge them to doubt their doubts and find the answers.

SECTION TWO

Community

In a Family, Presence Is More Important Than Attendance

J.R.

Most churches count attendance, but few churches count presence. Counting attendance isn't inherently wrong, but when it's the only thing that we count, it can be dangerous.

Many weeks at our church, we say to our leaders, "Look around. Who isn't here? Who do we need to follow up with to check in with them to find out how they're doing?" We've wanted to instill a family-oriented approach to church. This means caring for people as more than just numbers, making sure that they know that we've noticed when they're there—and especially when they're not.

One of the most significant metaphors used in the New Testament for church is family. And when it comes to family, presence matters. It's why we like to say that *presence is more important than attendance.* While attendance assumes a number, presence assumes relationship.

When it's been several weeks since I've seen a family in our church, I'll reach out and contact them, saying, "We've missed you. How are you all doing?" Sometimes people immediately go on the defensive, nervously offering some kind of reason why they've been gone the last few weeks—and I politely and tactfully try to interrupt them. I simply tell them I'm not here to ask them passive-aggressively why they haven't been at church. I simply tell them that I love their presence. I love that they're part of our church and that sincerely we've missed them. They relax.

To be clear, it's not that attendance is unimportant. In fact, presence may be *more* of a commitment than attendance. We challenge people to be all-in, committed in ongoing participation with the body of Christ—not just showing up for a Sunday morning service. If I sense that some of our longtime people have been slacking off, I approach them and say, "We've missed you all. Is everything okay with you?" They'll attempt to reassure me. "Oh, yeah, we've just been tired and busy the last few weeks. We just decided to sleep and catch up on rest"—thinking that that would satisfy. I often respond by saying, "Rest is good, I know full well. But we need you here. Your presence in this church matters, and as leaders you help set the tone here. When you slack off, people notice—and they begin to slack off, too. I'd like for you to consider making a deeper commitment to be present with us. When you're not present, we suffer. And when we are not present with you, you suffer. It's a part of being a family together, God's family." Presence provides greater care, but it also provides greater challenge—but it's worth it. Healthy communities are simultaneously high-grace and high-accountability contexts.

Hebrews says, "Let us consider . . . not giving up meeting together, as some are in the habit of doing, but encouraging one another—and all the more as you see the Day approaching" (10:24-25). The author of Hebrews was not simply attempting to convince people to show up to a Sunday service so they could report higher attendance on the weekly report. No, the author is stressing the importance of a deep commitment to accessibility and presence with God and one another.

In a family setting, when members of that family are missing, concerned people notice. The church should be no different. The role of leaders and shepherds in a local church isn't just to notice who is there; it should also include noticing who isn't there—and then lovingly reaching out to them in some way throughout the week. An older single woman in our church came down with the flu on a Saturday night and was unable to be with us in our gathering the next morning. She told me the following week, with tears in her eyes, how affirming it was to have several people from our church check in with her over the next few days to find out how she was doing. Meals were dropped off. Several called. A few people sent get-well cards. One family brought flowers. She told me, "This is what family does for one another. I love this church." When we notice people are missing and respond, we are making presence a higher priority than attendance.

Ultimately, our goal is not to get people to go to church. Our goal is to introduce people to the love of God, which is done best in the midst of a loving community. We need one another in the body of Christ. With presence as a higher value than attendance, the focus remains on growing hearts more than on growing numbers.

Community Is Made, Not Found

Bob

All too often I find myself sitting across from someone who is leaving our church, as he or she says, "I just haven't found community here." My follow-up questions are usually met with puzzled looks: "Have you joined a home group, or been a part of much [or indeed, anything] outside of Sunday mornings?" I don't ask because I'm genuinely wondering. Whenever I hear that someone hasn't "found" community, I know that the issue is often that someone hasn't made the effort, because *effort* is what it takes.

That's why in our welcomes on Sunday, in our new peoples' groups and in whatever other way we can, we try to tell people that community is something you make, not something that someone else can hand to you or that you accidentally stumble across. We do try to make it as easy as possible for folks—introducing them to others we think they might hit it off with, recommending home groups for them to check out. But when it comes down to it, the responsibility to create community rests on the individual looking for it.

This is hard for many to hear, especially introverts and those who have been hurt in past church situations. It's really difficult to put yourself out there and risk relationship knowing that it might not work immediately, or that there's a cost involved. People who have recently graduated from college, or who have come from parachurch or missions organizations where community seems baked in to the experience, find this especially hard to come to grips with. And believe me, if I could somehow create the elusive thing people are looking for and hand it to them at the door, I would. But I can't. And neither can you.

And that's why it's imperative to remind people that they will have exactly the amount of community that they are working for, or at least willing to receive when others invite them into it with invitations to be a part of various parts of church life. We have to encourage people that community takes work. Perhaps for them it will take laying aside the suspicions that these people here are like those people *there*, the ones who hurt them previously. Perhaps it just means helping them to ratchet down expectations that community comes easily or quickly.

I really feel for those who find it difficult. As an introvert myself, the last thing I want to do is walk into a situation where I know no one, where relationships have already been formed and I am joining the story midact. And so when I am reminding others that community is made, not found, I'm often reminding myself.

Don't scare people away with dire warnings that community is elusive and difficult. Just remind them that it takes time and purposeful effort. Welcome them warmly and do whatever you can to help them connect, but always let them know that, without effort on their part, over a decent amount of time, what they are seeking will remain out of reach. And it will be that way as long as they view community as something they hope to find in your church, and not something they are determined to create.

When We Put on Our Masks, We Put Aside the Cross

J.R.

The four-letter f-word is uttered in numerous churches each Sunday morning—and nobody seems to care all that much.[1] We keep using it, and nobody is confronting the problem. That four-letter *f*-word is *fine.* "How are you doing?" "Oh, I'm fine."

It's easily accessible and the most-used mask in the church today. It can be heard dozens of times each week on Sunday morning. There are times when we say this when we are not fine—and we know it. Others may know it, too, but we get a pass. How often are the regular Christian clichés we use nothing more than mere disguises of our hurt and pain, keeping us from sharing how we are *really* doing? Maybe most dangerous of all, we may eventually fool ourselves into thinking we're actually okay.

Sadly, even in the church—a place built upon grace—it can be difficult to actually find grace. Scores of pastors have confided in me, expressing their fear of being themselves with the people God has entrusted to their care. They are fearful. And fear drives us to create and fasten masks. Masks are nothing more than emotional armor seducing us to believe we will remain unscathed. Many of us have learned to adapt our behaviors in creative and sometimes subtle ways with motivations rooted in protecting ourselves from future exposure pain. The deeper the fear, the more creative we can be in our mask-making abilities.

As pastors we have our own set of unique masks we are tempted to wear:

- *The "I'm the Strong One" mask:* "I have what it takes to be the super-pastor you want me to be."
- *The "I'm Theologically Educated" mask:* "My seminary training and mastery of biblical languages prepares me for any situation."
- *The "I'm Spiritually Mature" mask*: "I can handle any circumstance and will keep it together because Jesus is on my side; I am the pastor, after all."
- *The "I'm Not Hurt" mask:* "God's grace is sufficient, and therefore I can convince you I'm all right."
- *The "I'm Just Like Everyone Else" mask:* "I may serve as a pastor, but I'm just a normal person like you."
- *The "I'm Super Busy" mask:* "I really wish I could, but I just have too much going on right now."
- *The "I Only Struggle with the Little Petty Sins" mask:* "I am a sinner, but I only struggle with 'respectable' sins."[2]
- *The "See How Vulnerable I Am" mask:* "I'm willing to share only some parts of my life with you where I'm less than perfect."

We reach for masks most often and most easily when our own livelihood is threatened.[3] Masks are emotional invisibility cloaks, pastoral coping mechanisms and emotional crutches shielding us from vulnerability, numbing our pain and keeping us from the thing we need the most: *grace*. We preach God's unconditional love, and yet we live by religion's conditional arrangement.

Author Madeleine L'Engle wrote, "If we refuse to take the risk of being vulnerable, we are already half-dead."[4] Jesus used a unique word to address those who were playing at religion: *hypocrites*. In Greek culture, hypocrites were theater actors who wore oversized masks so people sitting far away could see facial expressions during scenes. Hypocrites, quite literally, are mask-wearing play actors performing on the stage.

When are we most tempted to reach for our masks? When we are (or perceived to be) judged by others, when we don't have all the answers or when others offer us clear opportunities to wear them? What may be helpful for us next time we are tempted to reach for a mask is to try to identify the underlying emotions that exist in us: "Am I fearful? Numb? Uncertain? Am I trying to cover the pain? Do I feel shame? If so, why? What is the source of my lack of trust in the cross, which shattered any need to go reaching for a mask in the first place?"

Dallas Willard said, "Eliminate pretending from your repertoire. That will be wonderfully helpful in becoming the kinds of leaders the world desperately needs."[5] When we put on our masks, we put down the cross. But conversely, when we pick up the cross, we must put down the masks. If we continue to reach for masks, grace will never be essential to our lives; it will simply remain optional. As long as the masks remain, the loneliness remains.

When masks come off and the gospel is put on, when brokenness is acknowledged, grace is on the doorstep. As N. T. Wright wrote: "You don't need masks or makeup in the kingdom of God."[6] And that is very good news.

Come as You Are, but Don't Stay as You Are

J.R.

We only have one rule at our church: *no perfect people are allowed.*[1] Since our inception we've adopted a posture of "come as you are," making great efforts to communicate to those who visit our church that you don't have to clean yourself up in order to explore what a life with Christ looks like. Doctors aren't for healthy people but for the sick (which is one of Jesus' most well-known mantras).

In the first few years of our church's existence, people loved this one-rule concept of *no perfect people are allowed.* People loved telling others. We embraced it fully; many newcomers felt at ease knowing this was our posture.

But over time we realized we had a problem on our hands. Our leaders noticed something unnerving: people—many who had grown up in church most of their lives—thought that we were giving them an excuse to *remain as they were.* They embraced "come as you are," but they embraced "stay as you are," too. They completely missed the role of spiritual maturity, sanctification and holiness in the life of a follower of Christ. They perceived that our church was giving them an excuse to remain spiritually stagnant. When we challenged them directly, they bristled. When we confronted areas of sin, they would respond, "I thought we are a 'come as you are' church." What they were saying, in a sense, was "I thought we could basically do what we want here and everyone would be okay with that." They assumed we were giving them a spiritual "get out of jail free" card. (They assumed incorrectly.)

While God meets his people where they are, he most certainly does not desire for his people to stay where they are. We never want to communicate that our church is soft on sin, and we never desire to give people an excuse to do as they please. What we had assumed—but never clearly articulated—was that if you come as you are, Jesus will meet you there. But we had also assumed that people understood that the closer we get to Jesus, the more he requires of us. In fact, he requires that we come and die with him. But the closer we get to Jesus, the more he frees us, too.

We knew we needed to communicate more clearly. Yes, this is a "come as you are" church. But, the more we encounter Jesus and learn about his character, the more we receive his grace and the more we grasp what he asks of us as his followers, the less we can stay as we are. Using this mantra regularly helped clarify our expectations and articulate what Jesus requires of each one of us who are in relationship with him. We could correct false assumptions about easy discipleship and what Bonhoeffer called cheap grace. We also raised the bar of urgency and articulated the need for accountability. And we could say unabashedly that life change is what we are about as a local church family.

To be a Jesus community that cares about the process of people being spiritually formed means embracing all sorts of people—while also anticipating that people will change as they encounter the life-altering person of Jesus. In essence we are saying, "We will meet you where you are now, but we long to journey with you to where Jesus wants you to be in the future."

As Dietrich Bonhoeffer wrote, "To encounter God is to change."[2]

We're Different Because You Are Here—but You Need to Tell Us How

Bob

Have you ever discovered that someone you've known for years harbors a secret talent? One thing that has consistently amazed me in church life is how many people are hiding their talents, gifts and abilities. Some do so for the simple reason that they don't want anyone else to know. Maybe they use this particular set of skills all week long in their jobs, and the last thing they want is a repeat performance on Sunday. But the ones that really surprise me are those who keep their talents hidden and yet somehow manage to be upset that those talents aren't being better used in the church community.

For this reason, and a couple of others, we developed the mantra "We're different because you are here—but you need to tell us how." Our encouragement to people is not to let years go by before they begin to figure out where their gifts meet the community's needs. It's a tricky thing to encourage people to tell you what they are good at, as people's perceptions of their own talents sometimes lack a certain amount of objectivity. Nonetheless, we want people to know we want them—all of them, their gifts and talents, their time and who God has made them to be—for the greater good of the whole community.

Emphasizing how each individual changes the community with his or her presence presents a number of benefits. First, it helps people to think of themselves as a part of the community from day one. There's no inner clique that needs to be broken into—as soon as you walk through the doors, you change, in some small way, who we are as a community. Repeatedly saying this aloud to the community helps people to take ownership much more quickly.

Second, it encourages people to understand that when they are missing, or if they leave, there's a hole in the community shaped exactly like them. No one is expendable in the body of Christ (though as leaders, we're certainly tempted to think that way sometimes). Everyone leaves a gap when they go, and we feel it not only when people move away and are no longer able to be a part of our church, but also when people fade away and just stop being present for unknown reasons.

Third, it fights the subtle, yet real, misconception that, at a certain point, we arrive. We've got all the people we need, and more people will just mean more problems, more work and so on. It's a perspective that is hardly ever voiced, but it's present. When a church begins, every person that walks through the door feels like a gift from God. But as the church reaches a certain level of stability, leaders must fight the mindset that "we're all here now." More, we have to remind folks that who we are as people, though we hold certain central truths tightly, can change as new people show up. Who we are now is not who we will be a year from now. This is how God grows and matures our community as he brings new folks along. We can look back fondly on the days when things were smaller and more easily managed, but to try to stay in that place, or to long to go back to it, shows a misunderstanding of the fundamental mission of the church.

This is another mantra that gets used consistently in our welcomes on Sundays as well as in our new people's group. We want people to begin to take initiative within the community as quickly as possible, to volunteer, to pitch in and lend a hand where needed, or to bring something we didn't even know we needed. Every person who walks into our church is a gift, no matter what our size.

Stare at the Black Lines in Front of You

J.R.

It's amazing what the black lines on the butt of an impala can teach you about biblical community.

Several years ago my wife and I had the privilege of leading a group of young adults on a mission trip to South Africa and Mozambique. On our day off, our hosts took us to a game reserve in the northern part of South Africa. Our guide, Andre, drove us through the bush to encounter wild African game. No fences, gates or razor wire—our safari vehicle was the only thing between us and elephants, warthogs, giraffes, wildebeests, impalas, kudu, antelope and zebras.

Andre told us that many of the animals are always on alert, constantly on the lookout for predators. The impala (somewhat of a mix between a deer and an antelope, not the vehicle) has two parallel, vertical black lines on its rear end. When a predator (mostly the lion) attacks a group of impalas, the impalas stay together in one group. Their brains, on high alert, can think only one thing: *Stare at the black lines of the butt in front of me!* In a time of threat, they stay together by keeping their eyes focused on those black lines and follow closely enough with the others. The lion becomes confused, not knowing which one to attack. Eventually, it tires and gives up the hunt. If impalas run together, they stay alive; if they take their eyes off of the black lines of the butt in front of them and stray from the pack, they're left exposed. Eventually, they are captured and eaten.

As I heard this story, I thought of 1 Peter 5:8: "Be alert and of sober mind. Your enemy the devil prowls around like a roaring lion looking for someone to devour." Sadly, and all too frequently, we've seen people venture out on their own and find themselves cornered by the Evil One and devoured. One of the Evil One's greatest tools is to whisper to us—oftentimes quite compellingly—*You are the only one. No one else is struggling with what you're struggling with. You are a freak. And you can't tell anyone else about it.* It's at that moment that the lion is hunting down a lone impala. It's only a matter of time before it's over.

As a way to counter one of Satan's greatest tools, God gives us a gift called the church—a group of God's people who each have two parallel black lines on their rear ends. The local church becomes the place where we learn to stare at the black lines of the people in front of us (metaphorically, of course), while also faithfully modeling the same for the rest of the community and inviting them to stare at the black lines on our butts.

We live into God's best when we seek his kingdom above all else while running with others in obedience. When we stay together, we reduce exposure to the work of the Evil One. Christianity is a team sport. Stare at the black lines in front of you. As God's people, may we never run alone.

It's Only When You're Vulnerable That You Grow

J.R.

I was convinced there was no way it could be true. As a skeptical sophomore at Taylor University, I first heard this mantra from an upperclassman named Jon Cavanaugh. I spent months wrestling with that phrase, thinking about my life and all the ways in which I have grown. I finally realized Jon was right—every time I've grown and matured it was preceded by vulnerability. Few statements affected me more significantly during college than this one, and I've repeated it countless times since. Jon and I have become good friends, and he now serves as the chaplain at Taylor. When I see him, I remind him just how important that phrase has been in my life and how often I repeat it.

The good news of the gospel is found in our vulnerability, weakness and brokenness; it is by our willingness not only to express but also to embody our vulnerability that Jesus is able to do his best work in and through us.

In our relationship with God, vulnerability and growth are inseparable. When I'm vulnerable with other people—whether it is my wife or a friend or someone in our church—it releases something significant in my soul. It moves us closer to each other. It helps to remove the tumors of self-sufficiency in my life. Truly, when we are vulnerable, we risk being hurt. Vulnerability can, at times, feel excruciating. But it can be a meaningful gift. Vulnerability is the path that makes meaningful connection with God and others possible.

In speaking with those who've attended our church, there are many people—especially men—who come in with the wrong mindset that they must be strong in all situations: a mindset that believes that the "American way" of self-sufficiency can be held simultaneously with our passionate pursuit of Christ. But I quickly remind them that it was Jesus' vulnerability—his suffering and crucifixion—that made a way possible for us to have a life with Christ.

For growth to occur, vulnerability must be present. There is not a single time in our lives when we have ever grown, or will ever grow, without first being vulnerable—biologically, relationally, emotionally, spiritually.

We may not like this reality, but it is true. The sooner we come to grips with vulnerability and enter into it in appropriate and courageous ways, the sooner we will realize that it's not a curse, but a blessing.

If You're Not Hurt, Get off the Bench!

Bob

My son Jack's football team has a tradition that the entire team—even those on the sidelines—are active participants in the game. Each player is expected to stand on the sidelines, pay attention and cheer on their teammates throughout the entire game. One week, the coach turned around, noticed a few players sitting on the bench and yelled something that grabbed my attention: "If you're not hurt, get off the bench!"

Our church community has always done its best to welcome those hurt by life, by other church experiences or even by their own choices, and to give them time and space to heal. Healing from hurt is a work God often does in us through community. This is a valuable ministry that I'm not sure all churches engage in.

Too often church communities are either in the "Let's pay someone to do all of the work that needs to be done" mindset or in the "Everyone needs to be doing something right now" mindset. We've tried a different approach. We see relief on many faces when we say to the congregation, "This may not be your season to serve. If you come here hurt, burned out and in need of healing, just *rest*."

But at a certain point, it's important to encourage people to realize that resting eventually becomes stagnation. Whether it's hosting or leading home communities or other small groups, helping with setup on Sundays, or volunteering in the kids' room, it's all vital to the mission of our communities to be the kind of places where people can not only rest but find Jesus, and not only heal but also grow in the service of God and others.

While we continue to invite those who are healing to rest and find what they need in our churches, we also challenge others to provide what's needed. We want them to see church not as simply for themselves, but for others and for a broken and hurting world; and we want them to find their role in creating the kind of community that they—and hurt and broken people—need.

Challenge people to rest when needed, to heal when needed, but also to remember: "If you're not hurt, get off the bench!"

Let Your Needs Be Known

Bob

"We need help with our marriage."

"I need someone to help me figure out what Jesus means to me."

"I don't know how to hear God, but I want to."

"We have an emergency financial need . . ."

Believe it or not, these are all phrases I wish I heard *more* as a pastor.

While people aren't shy about complaining, or asking for little things, when it comes to what is truly important in life—what *really* matters—people seem to have a much harder time asking for help. For that reason, one of the mantras we try to use often is "Let your needs be known."

First, notice we're talking about needs, not wants. We're not inviting people to become more proactive church consumers. Lord knows we don't need any more of those! But we do want to give people permission and encouragement to bring to the attention of pastors, elders, other trusted people in the church or the church community as a whole what is really going on in their lives and what they really need from the rest of us.

One of the most heartbreaking things we face as pastors is when marriages hit the skids, and we hear about it secondhand or even later and only then are able to come and offer help. By that time, it is often too late. Or when people leave the church saying something like, "We really couldn't find what we needed here." If only they had asked!

The truth is, leaders aren't mind readers, and we'll never know what people need in their individual lives and with their individual struggles unless they tell us. Sure, we get pretty good at guessing.

But often, we miss the real needs because they are hidden behind silent, smiling faces, and we only find out after the fact that there was a question, struggle or deep desire of the heart that was going unmet. That leaders aren't mind readers would seem to be common sense, but I find it's something we need to remind people of pretty regularly. It's not that they think we are, but too often people assume we know what's going on with them or inside of them when, in truth, we haven't got a clue.

Another reason we use this mantra is a little less obvious. By letting your needs be known, you actually serve the community as a whole by letting others serve you. There are people in the church who are skilled counselors, and while they can't provide therapy to people they are in community with, they are certainly willing to sit down over coffee and listen, and perhaps help by talking things out. There are people who are talented carpenters, electricians or plumbers who don't play an instrument, or don't feel like the kids' room is really their area of expertise, but are happy to help those around them with whatever disaster of home repair that has befallen them, *if only people would ask.* The thing with people who long to serve others is they need to know there's a need before they can move to fill it. And when no one is asking, they can often feel as if they are of little or no use to the community.

Letting your needs be known and allowing others to use their gifts to serve you can be humbling. It's hard to admit you don't have it all figured out or are facing an issue you need help with. But this is one way that God forms us; particularly, it is how he forms humility in us.

Invite your church to let their needs be known—to leaders, to individuals they think might be able to help or to the church as a whole. Because when that happens, we begin to create a culture of authenticity, where people can be real, and a culture of service, where all people find opportunities to use their gifts.

This Community Will Be What You Make It

Bob

In the beginning days of a church, everyone takes ownership. The people who are helping to start a church almost universally see it as "theirs" and see themselves as coworkers laboring side by side to help create a new community. As time wears on, however, the amount of ownership new people feel decreases, as more and more begin to see the community as something they "attend." People who come in year five tend to feel differently than people who come in week five because they are joining something that already has a shape, an ethos and a way of doing things.

The problem with ownership is that it's rarely something that people just take or assume on their own. It needs to be constantly reinforced and renewed in the hearts and minds of the people who are part of your community.

One of the ways we have tried to help people take ownership of the community and what happens (or fails to happen) in it is by regularly using the mantra "this community will be what you make it."

We want people to see that the burden of making the community something that honors God and invites others in, that serves the needs of the people who are in it and the city around it, belongs to everyone, not just the pastors, elders or other leaders. Too many people have had too many experiences in too many churches that seek to do everything for them. Perhaps under the auspices of "excellence" everything begins and ends with paid staff that ensure that all things run smoothly.

I once worked in a church that had a fantastic building-services department. They not only took care of the grounds and maintenance of the church building, but they also set up chairs and tables for any group that wanted to use a room for a meeting. My wife worked as the administrator in the department and would regularly get calls saying, "We asked for fifteen chairs, but there are only ten set up—could someone come down and set up five more?" The chairs were right there in the closet, in the room, and yet the expectation was that someone would come, drag them out and set them up so the meeting could begin. The executive pastor cast a vision for the department that they would act as a "concierge service" for the church—and the church certainly treated them that way.

That's a small example of a lack of ownership in a church community, but to me it's telling of an overall mindset that can be created in a community when the expectation that only certain people (usually paid) do certain things begins to creep in.

One of the benefits of encouraging overall ownership in the community is that things *just happen*. There are many times when something awesome shows up in our community, and I have no idea who is responsible. Whether it's the coffee we need every week, the occasional donuts for before the gathering, artwork or prayer stations for the community, or book discussion groups, I have no idea who is starting and providing all these wonderful things on a regular basis. People see needs, have great ideas and are just moved to do something, all because they feel ownership of the community as a whole and feel empowered to act.

The shape, ethos and "way of doing things" in a community is something that ought to be watched over and guarded by the leadership, but held in trust by the community as a whole. If everyone is given ownership, the community actually becomes self-policing. This far into our journey together as a church, there's definitely an "Evergreen Community way" of doing things, and people just seem to intuit it and pass it on to others as they come. Even in year ten or twenty, a church is still "becoming," still growing up in Christ into who and what they will be, and it's the responsibility of everyone to help it do so.

Reminding people that "this community will be what you make it" takes the burden off of the shoulders of leadership. It helps people to see that no matter who they are, or what their gifts might be, they play a vital role and bear ultimate responsibility for what the church does, or fails to do.

It's Not Community Until It Gets Hard

Bob

Church is easy—at least when everything is going right. Many Christians—especially those under thirty-five—tell us often that what they long for more than anything else is authentic community. On the surface, this sounds wonderful. But dig a little deeper, and you'll often find that their assumptions and presuppositions are based around their own personal preferences and opinions. When those preferences aren't being met, they can be quick to leave and try to find them elsewhere.

Church is not a Fantasy Football team, where we have the opportunity to pick from the best options and assemble them into an ideal community. God calls us to love the *real* church, not the fantasy church—and real community isn't born out of successes and good times. It's born out of those hard times that require all members to reassess and reaffirm their commitment, not only to God and his church, but to the particular church community of which they are a part—the real flesh-and-blood people around them who are struggling to see their way through disappointment, failures and pain.

Dietrich Bonhoeffer offered a harsh warning about our view of biblical community: "Those who love their dream of a Christian community more than they love the Christian community itself become destroyers of that Christian community even though their personal intentions may be ever so honest, earnest and sacrificial."[1] Healthy biblical community is forged in moments when people are forced by circumstance to look at one another and say, "We are together in this." It's solidified in those times during which we begin to wonder if it's all worth it, only to come back to the enduring promises of Jesus—that we *would* face trouble and hard times, that we would have our unity tested, but, perhaps most importantly, he would be with us through it all. Community becomes real when we look around and say, "I don't like this tension we are struggling through right now. I don't even like some of these people right now! But I love them—and more, I am *with* them."

Jesus' approach to community is quite unexpected. Have you ever noticed how Jesus was really good at making awkward community work? He seemed to be able to bring together the left-outs, the dropouts, the mess-ups and the ignored and make something beautiful out of the group. But have you also noticed that Jesus was good at making working community awkward? When things are going smoothly, he seems purposefully to throw a wrench in the whole thing. He not only welcomes the mess; he at times seems to initiate it.

But if the church is the place for hurting and hungry sinners, it means we can expect it to get messy. It's something we need to hear when we are in the middle of the dark valleys. It's also something we need to hear when the road ahead looks clear and even—because hearing it, knowing it and keeping it top of mind can help us, when the inevitable bumps come, to be formed through them rather than derailed by them. In fact, if community is always easy and fun, we are either in denial or we haven't yet spent enough time together.

As I write these words, I am in the midst of a family vacation that so far has been an absolute disaster: massive car problems, unexpected delays and incessant rain. We are faced with the real question as to whether or not we're going to arrive at our destination at all. But in the midst of it all, I can see God forming something in us as a family—a bond and an appreciation for one another, for what we *do* have—that might otherwise have been missed had everything gone according to plan.

It's the hard times that bring a family together, and it's the hard times that change a church into a community.

SECTION THREE

Formation

Everything Is Formation

Bob

In Eugene Peterson's wonderful autobiography, *The Pastor*, he quotes a poem by Denise Levertov, and her phrase, "Every step an arrival."[1]

Every choice we make, no matter how small or seemingly inconsequential, is actually another brick in our character formation, another piece of who we are becoming. Actions become habits; habits easily become character; character inevitably becomes destiny. Every step I take is an arrival at who we are becoming.

I remind myself of this when I am procrastinating. Exercise is formation—but so is *not* exercising. This also helps guide me when I consider giving of my time or money. I know I *want* to be a generous person (eventually), but in the moment, when I'm not feeling generous, I need to be reminded that the choice before me is forming something in me, *even as I am making it.*

Recently, I was talking to a younger pastor who struggles at times in his ministry context at a larger, more traditional suburban church. As I explained to him the idea that everything is formation, I could see a change come over his face. Whereas he had come into our conversation seeing his struggle with his church's position on the role of women in ministry, their reluctance to listen to his ideas, and an overconcern with money coupled with an underconcern for building deeper spirituality in the staff and even the congregation as a soul-sucking burden that was making him want to cut and run, slowly he began to understand that his reaction to these frustrations was going to work one of two things in him: either bitterness or a deeper formation. Either he would continue to become more and more angry about the situation, or he would begin to see how all of these issues could form something in him—a deeper appreciation for the struggle of women who desire to minister to others, the ability to think long-term and have the patience required for change, a passion for prayer and for encouraging others to pray. He began to see others on staff not as those who were opposing him, but as those who were helping to form him, even if it was only by bringing into sharper focus for him how he *didn't* want to pastor. He began to see the problems he was experiencing in the church as ways God was beginning to shape his views and passions.

We especially encourage our church to see all that we do together as a community as formation, and to give themselves to it with the energy that something that forms our hearts and souls deserves. We are not just reading Scripture together on Sundays; we are being formed. We are not just singing songs, listening to a sermon, making small talk with others. We are being formed and are participating in the formation of others. In that light, it's all worthy of our full attention, best efforts and total presence.

All of life is formation, not just the parts that might seem more "spiritual." How we listen to others, how we treat them, the presence we give them or fail to give them—all of these things are shaping us, slowly but surely, into who we will be.

Every step is an arrival. Everything is formation.

Follow the Lights on the Runway

J.R.

Countless times people have asked me, "How can I understand what God wants me to do with my life?" In my response, I remind them that discerning God's purposes for their futures is not a code to be hacked into; it's not a nut to be cracked or a "problem" to be solved. It is an opportunity. The process of discerning God's best for our lives is one of the most effective means to draw closer to him.

In this opportunity, there are means to God's guidance. I tell them to *follow the lights on the runway.* (It was the advice that I was given by mentor Tom Yeakley when I was just starting out in ministry.)

If you've ever driven past a small airport at night, you can't see the runway on the other side of the chain-link fence. There is, however, a brief moment when all the lights on the runway line up momentarily as you're passing by. These indicators point pilots in the proper direction for takeoff or landing. Similarly, God gives us five lights on our runways by which to discern his purposes for our lives.

Light 1: Scripture (see Psalm 119:105). Is there anything in God's Word that would indicate that this is wise and good or dishonoring or sinful?

Light 2: Personal peace when praying (see Philippians 4:6-7). The bold truth is that if given enough time, I can rationalize just about anything in my mind. But when I'm in committed and earnest prayer with the Lord, it's difficult for me to do that. Sometimes in my time of prayer, my soul feels unsettled, like swirling snow in a shaken snow globe. However, there are times in prayer that usher in a peaceful presence regarding a decision, like when all of the snow eventually settles to the bottom of the snow globe.

Light 3: Wise counsel from other believers (see Proverbs 15:22). God gives us the gift of the church. This includes wise, committed followers of Jesus in community. We see throughout the Scriptures that God speaks to others and through others about his purposes. Seeking out wise counsel of a handful of people who love the Lord and want what's best for us—and looking for themes, trends or common threads that run throughout—can be wise.

Light 4: Wise thinking (see 1 Peter 1:13; James 1:5). God gave us a brain, and he wants us to use it. One of the ways that we love God with all of our minds is by thinking wisely and critically about issues. Sometimes, for example, that involves making a list of pros and cons to consider all the options. We need to trust God's promise that he not only wants to give us wisdom if we ask, but also that he will do it faultlessly and generously.

Light 5: Providential circumstances (see Revelation 3:7-8). God intervenes and works in the everyday situations of humans. God's already-at-work-behind-the-scenes grace and timing are perfect—and sometimes can almost feel eerie. Some may see coincidences, but what if they were hints, shadows or promptings of God's presence in our lives?

When these five lights begin to line up in a relatively straight line, we can move forward with confidence believing there is a runway from which we can land or take off. Conversely, if the lights on the runway are zigzagged, we should feel less confident that this is God's purpose for our lives.

A word of caution: don't rely too heavily on only one or two lights. Some people find a verse to support just about anything that they want; others can have "peace" about anything or find counsel to tell them what they want to hear. Certainly, this is not a surefire equation; nor is it five easy steps to knowing God's will. But together these runway lights can be a tool to help us lean in further toward the heart of God.

And remember the importance of waiting for God's timing (see Hebrews 10:36). *The right thing done the wrong way can easily become the wrong thing.* The more these lights line up in the same direction, the more confident we can be that God is leading us in this direction—but ultimately we must wait for clearance to land and take off.

Be Childlike, but Don't Be Childish

J.R.

"Be as shrewd as snakes and as innocent as doves" (Matthew 10:16)—another one of Jesus' compelling mantras.

In today's culture, to be shrewd is to be cunning, manipulative or deceitful, in order to gain the upper hand. We might think of a shady businessperson, a used-car salesman or a crooked attorney. With this understanding, we can be left confused by Jesus' words.

Yet *shrewd* actually means to have or show sharp powers of judgment; it means to be astute. People who are shrewd use every opportunity to its maximum potential. I've known people who are pure in heart and upright in character, but who aren't "street smart." They act aloof, are easily taken advantage of and don't possess a lot of wisdom. I've also known people who are shrewd in particular situations, adept in making numerous connections, able to open up doors of opportunity and to work hard to make things happen. But I observed them telling the truth, plus or minus ten percent. I learned their character was in serious question and they lacked integrity.

Jesus tells his followers to use every opportunity available, but to do it with a pure heart. Why? Because he was sending his followers out like sheep among wolves.

Paraphrasing Jesus' words, he encourages his followers to be childlike, but not childish. Jesus seems to assert his listeners: "Grow up! Think! Be wise! Use your brain!" Yet he also tells us that unless we become like little children, we have no part in the kingdom of God.

Here are helpful questions to ponder as we seek to find the shrewdness-innocence balance:

- *Shrewdness:* How can I take full advantage of this situation? How might I make connections, build bridges, deepen trust and maximize the opportunity here? What's the big picture? What implications does this situation have on the future?
- *Innocence:* What is my motive? Is there anyone who might question my character if he or she knew all angles of this opportunity? Am I seeking to leverage this situation to my own selfish advantage, or do I want this to benefit others? How might my actions, motivations and desires honor others and glorify God?

So much of leadership is wisdom. We need wisdom to know the difference between childlikeness and childishness. And when kingdom leaders find the right shrewdness-innocence balance, we honor God's heart and the people we serve.

Don't Ask "Why?" Ask "What?"

Bob

"Consider it pure joy . . . whenever you face trials" (James 1:2) is one of Scripture's easiest commands to repeat, to ourselves and others, and yet one of the hardest actually to practice.

James' reasoning is that God works through our suffering to form us, to work in us "perseverance" (James 1:3) or a "patient endurance." The word he uses for perseverance or endurance, depending on your translation, is *hypamenō*, or literally "to remain under." It describes the strength of character and fortitude it takes to remain under a great weight, or under suffering. James says that we ought to let this patient endurance finish its work in us, its work of making us mature in Christ.

Paul says much the same thing in Romans 5:3-4, when he says we can rejoice when problems and trials come our way, because we know that they help us develop endurance, which helps us develop a strength of character, and that character strengthens our hope in God.

Both biblical authors have a formational view of trials and suffering. The view they took, and the view we ought to take, is that God can and does use the hard places in life to develop in us something that otherwise might go undeveloped.

All too often, when we hit a rough patch in life, the first question we ask God is, "Why is this happening to me?" We assume that in some way God is behind it, wanting to teach us a lesson or punish us for some sin. And if only we can puzzle out the "why" of it, we'll have passed the test, and the trial will magically disappear. I'll leave aside for now the question of what God causes and what God merely allows and point instead to a more biblical question to ask in the face of suffering, and that's the question of "what." What can God develop in me through this? What piece of my character (or lack thereof) is being brought into focus by what I'm experiencing? What rough spots are being chiseled, and what weak spots are being challenged? In other words, the focus shifts from "How can I get this to stop?" to "How can I grow through this?"

This focus works in us the practical virtue the biblical writers encourage us can come from suffering: endurance, the ability to remain steadfast in the face of whatever might come our way. It includes a much more redemptive view of suffering, seeing the pain we experience in life not as meaningless but as an opportunity for something good to come in our lives that otherwise we might have missed. It also shifts our view of God from someone who, for some strange reason we can't quite work out, is causing us pain and bringing suffering into our lives, to being the One who is able to salvage something out of and redeem the pain we will inevitably face in life. And trust me, these two different views of God have two different results in our lives.

The challenge is to encourage people to ask the right question about their pain *before they are in the midst of it*. People who are in the midst of suffering rarely are able to hear a theological framework of how we should view our own pain and trials. Mostly what they need is someone to listen, to pray with and for them, and to support them in any way possible. At the most, what I often do is open the door by asking where God has been in the midst of the pain, and perhaps what he's been bringing out of it. Asking open-ended questions like that is a much more pastoral way of helping people to think differently about their own suffering than simply telling them how I think they should handle things. It often happens that if people are willing to engage in those questions, as they think about them, their follow-up questions and comments frequently make room to explain a bit more about how God can use suffering to form and shape us.

In your own life, and as you pastor others, forgo asking "Why?" and instead ask "What?" "God, what good can you bring out of this? How can you use this circumstance to make me more like your Son, Jesus?"

Few Things Mess with Your Theology More Than Reading Your Bible

J.R.

The more I read my Bible, the more it messes with me. This is a good thing. I need to be messed with.

Engaging with Scripture—and specifically the Gospels—can be a detox program to help us flush out our damaging views of Christianity and our inaccurate thoughts about Jesus. Too often we seek to tame the Scriptures, putting them into nice, tidy categories. The Bible is clear and comforts me in times of distress, worry and confusion. But the Bible is also messy, confounding and baffling. I'm often left perplexed. I've learned this isn't a bad thing. But the Bible—the wild, wonderful, clear, powerful, mysterious story that it is—is something that needs to be unleashed and not be feared.

Dorothy Sayers famously wrote:

> The people who hanged Christ never, to do them justice, accused him of being a bore—on the contrary, they thought him too dynamic to be safe. It has been left for later generations to muffle up that shattering personality and surround him with an atmosphere of tedium. We have very efficiently pared the claws of the Lion of Judah, certified him "meek and mild," and recommended him as a fitting household pet for pale curates and pious old ladies.[1]

Certainly, sound biblical interpretation and guidance from the Holy Spirit are needed in studying and applying Scripture to our lives.

Paul instructs Timothy to pay special attention to his theology and doctrine. But that doesn't mean that our approach to theology and doctrine can't be messed with. As Scot McKnight has said, "Let's let the Bible be the Bible."[2] We need to let the Bible out of its cage so it can run wild.

We are called into a relationship with a God named Jesus who wants us to be Jesus-loving people free of religion. This is anything but tame. And once we make the choice to *live* the Scriptures, it forms how we actually read them.

We encourage people in our church when they read the Bible—whether they are seminary graduates or have never picked up a Bible before—to ask five questions:

1. What's going on in the passage?
2. What in the passage encourages and inspires me?
3. What in the passage offends, confronts, disrupts or challenges me?
4. What does this tell me about the nature of God, the character of Jesus or about the kingdom?
5. What am I going to do with what I've read in the next seven days?

What has surprised and encouraged me over the years is how many people resonate with the third question. Some have realized that their assumptions about God and his kingdom actually *contradict* what they read about in the Scriptures, which leads them to experience healthy unlearning.

It was Mark Twain who said, "It ain't the parts of the Bible that I can't understand that bother me, it's the parts that I do understand." And oftentimes, that's what messes with me the most.

SECTION FOUR

Conflict

Disagree Without Disengaging

Bob

Healthy community is not the absence of conflict, but the presence of Jesus in the midst of it.

When we say we want to be a community that is able to disagree without disengaging, we know we are fighting a tendency of the church in the last five hundred years that leads people who disagree with one another to form a fellowship with those who see everything the way we see it and cut ties with those who don't. Our Sunday gatherings are filled with both Democrats and Republicans. We know there are pro-gun folks and anti-gun folks. There is great diversity.

But in all of this, we call our church community to unity around the good news and the person of Jesus. It's not that we don't care whether or how people vote, or what causes they are involved in or think are a waste of time. There is something bigger taking place—and that can only happen when we don't merely tolerate those who are different from us, but actively lean into relationship with them, worship with them and love them in a Jesus-like way. This is the kingdom of God in all its glory, breaking down every dividing wall between people!

The ugly truth is that we are sinful and our sinful tendencies are bound to come out. When disagreements arise, we're tempted to split. But in the midst of our disagreements and sinful tendencies, we are given the opportunity to be a forgiving, reconciling, loving, serving, celebrating community. The other truth is this: *we are high maintenance.* The quicker we all acknowledge this truth, the easier it will be for us to receive the kind of grace Jesus wants to give to us individually and as a community, and in turn, we will extend that grace to others.

It's not all warm fuzzies, especially around election time, as emotions rise. We have to remind folks to be careful, not necessarily of what they say, as they are free to say and support whatever or whomever they'd like, but mostly of *how* they say it, and the respect with which they treat others who disagree with them. We have to remind folks that when they find someone in our community who thinks differently about a hot-button issue, or even when they discover that our leadership thinks differently than they about sexuality, money or any of a host of other things, it's not time to look for another church. It's time actually to lean in and listen, or, at the very least, acknowledge the diversity in our community and give up the false expectation that we will ever be completely in agreement about much of anything beyond Jesus and his good news.

People who cut and run at the first sign of doctrinal disagreement or social-issue differences will find themselves leaving one church after another, because there will always be people who see things differently. And even though they may find a church whose leadership agrees with them on the one issue they care about at the moment, eventually they'll discover other disagreements.

So, for their own sake, and for the sake of our community, we encourage people to see disagreement as a healthy sign of diversity within a community, and when they encounter it, not to disengage from the church or from the people with whom they are disagreeing. John Wesley said, "If your heart beats with my heart in love and loyalty to Jesus Christ, then take my hand."[1] When it comes to differences of opinion, let's not forget that there's a significant difference between acceptance and agreement. In the end, we believe that our best witness to the world is to be a community who can disagree in love and remain committed to one another—not because our political or social views bind us together, but because the expansive and reconciling love of Jesus is at work in all of us.

If You Feel Strongly Enough to Say Something About It, You're Probably Meant to Help Solve It

Bob

"I have a concern." Every church leader's favorite words! Throughout our early days we knew there were a lot of needs that were going unaddressed; things we intended to get to when we were able. Luckily, there were many in the community who, with keen perception, were able to see the places where we lacked, and were willing to say something about it.

To counter the perception that only pastors did work in the community, to help people take ownership of what was happening and what needed to happen in our new church, and frankly, to keep our own sanity, we developed this particular mantra.

Whenever people would say, "Have you thought about doing . . . ?" or "What really needs to happen . . . ," we would thank them for bringing something they clearly cared about to our attention. We would then suggest that because they cared about the issue and had eyes to spot what needed to be done, perhaps they were the ones who would best be suited to address the issue!

Of course, not everyone responded by jumping in feet first to solve whatever problem they had brought up. But many did. And as the word got out about how we responded to the things people brought up, two things began to happen.

First, those who just wanted to complain about things largely stopped doing so. Turning the issue back on people by asking what they thought needed to be done and then inviting them to do it made for much less complaining. People thought twice about casually bringing up a problem they had no intention of taking a hand in solving.

Second, people began to intuit our response before we even gave it. Sometimes, they'd still bring up the issue they were concerned about, but more out of seeking empowerment or permission to fix it. Other times, they would simply set about trying to find a solution on their own, and just tell us about it after they'd come up with something. Either response was one we wholeheartedly welcomed.

Consistently inviting people to solve the problems they see forms a culture of less complaining and more initiative in a church community. It helps people to see that those who have the title of leader in the church are not there to be a glorified concierge, but to equip and coach others as they do the work of ministry. And it helps pastors and leaders feel a lot less stress.

This is a mantra that we use mainly in conversation with people, but occasionally we'll repeat it during our welcomes on Sunday morning as we orient newer people into the community and remind longtime participants in the church of how we do things.

It's probably people's least favorite mantra, because it turns the tables and challenges them to take responsibility. But ultimately, an empowered community is *exactly* where we want to see the responsibility lie.

When You Fail, Don't Run

J.R.

One of Satan's strong messages to people is when you fail, run away and hide.

There are beautiful (yet rare) stories of people who choose to stay when people fail—either when they hurt others, or others hurt them. With all courage, compassion, faith and patience, they commit to work through the pain toward reconciliation and restoration. Yet, many avoid dealing with failure head-on and choose to leave. Many times they believe the pain and the shame are too much to deal with. They are spiritually malformed because they bypass the issue. They are conditioned to believe that running is acceptable, even normal.

In our church we talk about failure and conflict as *kairos* moments. There are two words in Greek for time—*chronos* and *kairos*. The Greeks used *chronos*—where we get our word *chronology*—to describe a specific measurement of time or a sequence of events (for example, 3:45 on a Tuesday afternoon). But *kairos* time is different. It describes a more qualitative reality. If *chronos* deals with clocks and calendars, *kairos* deals with moments and seasons. It is time pregnant with possibility, God's directed moments of invitation to deeper trust. *Kairos* time is rarely neutral; it leaves a mark on our lives, either positive or negative. *Kairos* times remain in our heads and hearts as some of our deepest, most lasting memories.

Our lives are measured by *chronos* time, but they are marked with *kairos* time—and each one of these moments elicit a response from us. More often than not, the biblical writers were describing time in the reality of *kairos*, not *chronos*. It's no wonder the biblical writers used *kairos* time almost twice as much as *chronos* time. The biblical characters saw *kairos* time as God-appointed moments in history—the in-breaking of God's activity. It is easy to focus our attention on *chronos* minutes so much that we miss *kairos* moments.

Failure is always a *kairos* moment. In fact, you will never experience a significant failure in your life that is not a *kairos* moment. Failure is a call, a challenge, an invitation and a test. How will we respond to *kairos* moments in *chronos* time? Wise followers of Christ steward *kairos* moments faithfully.

Healthy communities look to embrace *kairos* moments and learn from them, especially when they involve failure, pain or hurt. Jesus calls the church to be a giving, worshiping, loving, serving and forgiving family on earth that exemplifies the way of the kingdom. There's not a better place or family to work out failure-induced *kairos* moments than in the church, a place founded upon grace.

A middle-aged couple in our church was having significant marriage issues. When the wife learned that others knew of their troubles, she was ashamed to come to church. I ducked out of worship and found her in the hallway with red eyes and mascara all over her cheeks. She told me she was going to leave the church; she was just too embarrassed to stay. I told her she was too loved by too many to run right now. Plus, I told her that running would stunt her spiritual growth. She trusted me and stayed with our church—and her husband, too.

When we refuse to run but commit to sitting with others who've hurt us or whom we've hurt with a posture of humility and a desire for reconciliation, it models God's desire for his people. Some of the most beautiful stories in our church are when people chose to do the most excruciating thing possible by facing the hurt and failure and working through it instead of running. The beauty of reconciliation yields tears of joy. But sadly, we've also seen key leaders leave with a stubborn refusal to face up to the hurt; this has often brought tears of pain to our eyes, sometimes years later.

Think about it: in Acts 2 God used Peter in a dramatic way to communicate the message of world-saving hope just a few weeks after the greatest failure of his life. When you fail, make a commitment not to run. It may be incredibly difficult, but it's a *kairos* moment pregnant with the potential for deep, lasting and God-honored growth.

When you fail, honor God by stewarding *kairos* moments faithfully and wisely. You are too loved to run.

SECTION FIVE

Outreach

Be Missionaries Cleverly Disguised as Good Neighbors

J.R.

One of the primary roles of pastors is to develop a mindset in the people God has entrusted to them to be missionaries cleverly disguised as good neighbors.

When I think about the word *incarnation,* I remember back to learning about *chile con carne* in ninth-grade Spanish class—chili with meat. The incarnation was *God con carne,* when the God of the Universe wrapped himself in human flesh to be among us, as *Emmanuel.* "The Word became flesh and blood, and moved into the neighborhood" (John 1:14 *The Message*). And Jesus gives his followers the Holy Spirit and tells us to go be "little Christs"—*Jesus con carne*—out in the neighborhood.

In order to do this, as pastors we must grow to see ourselves as shepherds not simply of the people who attend our churches, but of our whole zip codes. It was John Wesley who said, "I look on all the world as my parish." If we embody an incarnational ministry posture, we begin to develop missionaries cleverly disguised as plumbers, attorneys, delivery-truck drivers, small-business owners, teachers, social workers, stay-at-home moms and union electricians—each with his or her own unique mission field and missionary context. (The only context where we discourage a missionary mindset is in dating situations.)

God is inviting us to join his mission. Thus, we have to ask a different set of questions. It's easy to ask, "How many people were there on Sunday?" But a missional mindset requires asking: "How are we blessing the neighborhood in the name of Jesus?" John Quick points out that we've missed the point if we can recite a thousand Bible verses but cannot recite our neighbors' names.[1] How would our kingdom imaginations be different if followers of Jesus only used the word *church* as a verb and *Christian* as a noun?

Oftentimes we ask this question in our church, "If we were not allowed to meet together on Sunday mornings, what would be left of our church?" And, "If our church had to shut its doors, would anybody mourn? Would anybody care? Or would anybody even notice?" These difficult but necessary questions are the types of questions that we keep in the forefront of our minds in order to think and act like missionaries.

When we were starting our church, we made a commitment that if we did not see evident kingdom activity Monday through Saturday *first*, then we would not launch a Sunday gathering. We believed gathering weekly for corporate worship was important, but we knew that the inertia of planning services week after week would force us inward if we did not make a commitment to be outward-focused all seven days a week first.

While this was extremely difficult for some in the short term, we made it clear from the start that this was an important part of our identity as missionaries in our context. We were not simply hoping to attract people to a highly excellent Sunday morning gathering in order to impress them or give them opportunities to spectate at a religious event. J. D. Greear writes that of the forty miracles recorded in the book of Acts, thirty-nine of them happened outside the walls of a religious building.[2] Let that sink in. See Sunday mornings as the pep rally at which to form, equip, inspire, educate and challenge people to live in the places that God has called them to embody Christ in the world—in the work room, in the playroom, in the boardroom or in the lunchroom.

These are difficult trade-offs. Many people come to a church expecting to receive goods and services. They expect the spiritual "paid professionals" (pastors) to do all the work for them in exchange for their dues (offerings). The temptations to pastors are present to be and do it all for those who attend. But these shortcuts now will eventually catch up to us later, when we would be creating a culture of religious consumerism.

We must resist the temptation to do it all; instead, we invest our lives in others in order to equip God's people for good works, as Paul wrote in Ephesians 4. Home Depot's old mantra works for churches, too: "You can do it. We can help." The church of Jesus Christ moves forward, as pastors and elders equip the congregation, while simultaneously refusing to do all the work for them. Eugene Peterson mused that a local church is a congregation of embarrassingly ordinary people in and through whom God chooses to be present in the world. When people—*all people*—are equipped to use their gifts, passions, skills, abilities and callings for God's purposes, they begin to live like missionaries in various mission fields all over the region. When God's people—even the embarrassingly ordinary ones—are committed to God's mission for God's glory seven days a week, you've got a church full of missionaries.

Belong Before You Believe

Bob

In his book *Reimagining Evangelism,* Rick Richardson coined the phrase "belonging comes before believing."[1] We have found it a useful mantra in encouraging people to dig into community, test the claims of Jesus and see what the good news of Jesus actually does in people.

We're aware that those who hold a high view of church membership are generally uncomfortable with the concept of allowing non-Christians full access to the community, as opposed to a more traditional membership-oriented community where only those who have put their faith in Jesus and assent to the doctrinal statements of the church are allowed true entrée. But we have genuinely felt that the benefits of membership (and they are many) don't quite outweigh the benefits of inviting people into community as a way of discovering Jesus, rather than as a reward for having done so.

When a non-Christian is allowed to be a full participant in a community and get an up-close look at what difference the gospel actually makes in people, he or she is given a front-row seat to the working of the Holy Spirit in our midst. Yes, you may want to have some sort of covenant or process that you ask people to take part in as they become Christians or want to commit fully to the church, but to say to people who don't yet know whether they want to give their lives to Jesus, "You can't serve here, and your voice will not be heard," is a quick way to shut down the process of their discovering whether or not Jesus is even someone they want to give their lives to.

While we reserve significant leadership for committed Christians, we do allow non-Christians to serve in most any other way; they have played music in our band, led justice ministries they were passionate about and served in the kids' room. This openness has resulted in many people giving Jesus a chance in their lives, and subsequently giving their lives to him.

I remember a time in our early years when we knew that we would have to move our Sunday gathering. We had outgrown the pub space we had started in, and the potential to rent part of a church building came up. We invited the whole community (yes, even the non-Christians) to pray and listen to God for direction as to what we ought to do.

In a meeting where everyone was invited to take part and be heard, we talked at length about the pros and cons of moving out of a more "public" space and into a more traditional church building. The tipping point in the discussion came when one woman, who probably wouldn't have identified at that time as a follower of Jesus, more just someone who was really interested in him and had a lot of questions, spoke up and said, "I don't think I ever would have come to this community had it been a church building." I looked around the room and saw many heads nodding; she had put into words the feelings of the majority of people in our church! More, even as a non-Christian, she had reminded us of why we existed as a church: to give people like her a place to explore faith. We decided to remain in nontraditional, public spaces and still do to this day. And it's been a huge open door to many, many people. I thank God for the presence of that non-Christian in our midst who reminded us of something important.

I once heard Erwin McManus say, "Every truly healthy church has two things: heretics and people who are sexually immoral." To translate, a church that consists only of committed Christians probably has lost sight of its mission and resembles more the "frozen chosen" than the messy community that God has in mind that journeys with people as they discover Jesus.

Invite people to belong to your community even before they believe, and to taste and see whether or not God really is good.

Don't Make Enemies Out of Words and Works

Bob

In recent years there's been an increasing divide between those who want to emphasize words (Scripture, doctrine and creeds) and those who see works as more important (justice, serving the poor, being Christ-like). I've often heard it said that it was better to be kind than to be right. Our question is *"Why wouldn't you want to be both?"*

I'm not sure when and where the recent battle of words versus works began. I suspect somewhere toward the end of the 1990s and the beginning of the twenty-first century, as there was a renewed emphasis on justice and deeper presence in neighborhoods and cities. And while we're certainly in favor of the church demonstrating the love of Christ and the good news of the gospel tangibly through its orthopraxy, I've always been mystified by the often attendant de-emphasis on orthodoxy.

In our community especially, I've seen this tendency. Younger Christians can tend toward being enamored of doing good, being kind, loving all, but less so of discovering the theological basis behind doing all of those things, or learning more about the God who calls them to do it, or the Jesus in whose name they act.

I take every chance I can when preaching and teaching to do away with this false dichotomy, encouraging people not to make enemies out of words and works. As Ron Sider said, we need both good news and good works. The creeds and doctrine alone are not sufficient. There have to be works behind them to show their impact and the way that God uses his truth to set people free. But works alone aren't sufficient either. It simply is not enough to be a good person, to be kind or to attempt to live like Jesus if we don't understand who he is, what he came to do, what he accomplished for us and what his kingdom is really about.

There have been times, as I've taken the pulse of our community, when I've realized we need to swing back in one direction or the other. If you've ever driven on a long, straight road, you know how hard it is to drive directly down the middle. There's constant steering correction happening, first this way and then that. In the aggregate, we go straight down the road and avoid the ditches on either side, but not without persistently giving the wheel slight nudges in both directions. In the same way, as you lead a community, you will go through times when what's being emphasized is right, missional living. I've found that without following those times with an emphasis on right belief, a community can veer too far in one direction and end up perilously close to the ditch. In this case, the ditch stands for proclaiming through how we live that being a Christian mostly has to do with being nice and kind, serving others and making the world a better place, and really has nothing to do with renewing our hearts, changing our minds and adjusting our actions (repentance). When some disciples asked Jesus what they needed to do "to do the works God requires," Jesus answered: "Believe in the one he has sent" (John 6:28-29).

We mentioned before Eugene Peterson's description of the Christian life as "a long obedience in the same direction." We would only add that it be the *right* direction.

I don't want to get hung up on doctrine, assigning the same weight to matters both big and small, as I'm sure that's part of the reason behind the de-emphasis in recent years. But without Scripture and right belief to inform our works, we're sure to end up in a ditch. It's not enough to be kind or good, and it's not enough to be right. We have to value and strive for each in equal measure.

Teach your community both. Don't make and don't let them make enemies out of words and works. Double major in good news and good works.

Rotate Your Crops

Bob

One of our goals as a community is to refuse to be the church that keeps people so busy they have no time for life outside of the church. We want to see lots of empty space on the calendar and encourage people to see their disposable time (time not spent at work, sleeping or with family) as a kingdom resource that ought to be spent with people from church *and* with people who don't know Jesus.

In an attempt to help people catch this mission mindset, and to keep them from getting burned out, we encourage them to rotate their crops.

Here's what we mean by that. We have three main avenues of engagement in our church beyond Sunday gatherings. You may have more, fewer or the same; the mantra works regardless. Our three are theology pubs (theology discussion groups that mostly meet in pubs) and discipleship huddles, home communities, and serving others (usually in some justice-related activity, but it could include working in the kids' room, serving on the worship team, etc.). We encourage people not to be doing more than two out of the three at any one time. So, for example, serve the homeless with us and be in a home community. After a season, maybe rotate out of serving and join a discipleship huddle or do that season's theology pubs. After another while, take a break from home community and begin serving again, perhaps in a new and different area.

As a farmer rotates crops between fields, letting a field rest after a couple of seasons of use, we hope crop rotation in our church keeps people from getting burned out on any one vital area.

Using this mantra also provides an opportunity for us to talk about all the different things happening in our community, and to give people permission to engage with them when the time is right. Further, it sets the expectation that, in spite of the fact that we don't want them doing too much, we do expect people to engage on some level beyond Sundays. We encourage our leaders to allow people to rotate in and out, and to watch for people who've been doing something too long and give them a break.

We recognize that this might vary in different church contexts. For example, the expectation for home communities may be 100 percent participation. I once heard a pastor say, "If you are not a part of a home group, you are not really a part of this church!" We think that's unrealistic for many in different seasons of life—those with a new infant, for instance, or those who live in a house with other singles who are truly living life and sharing generously with one another in God's honoring expressions of community. It also makes for overextended and stressed-out people who feel obligated to be in a home group, to serve in some area and to be in a discipleship or accountability group. Even though we have a smaller percentage of people involved in home communities than other churches, our hope is that by giving people permission to engage with something for a season, draw back and then reengage somewhere else, we safeguard the overall health of the people in our church. Over time, we see more well-rounded disciples of Jesus who have participated in the broad spectrum of what our church does together.

To be on mission with God means creating enough margin to be available to engage and live life with people who don't know Christ. Jesus made a lot of time for nonreligious people. We should, too.

SECTION SIX

Stewardship

Be a Pipe, Not a Bucket

J.R.

No one would ever accuse me of being handy around the house—not in the slightest. But I do know the difference between a pipe and a bucket.

What flows into a bucket, stays in the bucket.

What flows into a pipe, flows out of the pipe.

If water flows out of a bucket, there's a hole. Something's wrong.

If water doesn't flow out of a pipe, there's a clog. Something's wrong.

My knowledge impresses—I know.

We use this language of plumbing theology often in our church.[1] A passage that speaks to our calling as pipes is the parable of the talents (see Matthew 25:14-30). What the servants did with what was entrusted to them had a direct correlation to the master's response. Jesus' point is clear: he gets angry with those who—either out of fear or apathy—refuse to invest and keep it to themselves. He honors pipes and gets angry at buckets.

God, who has loved us outlandishly and generously, pours out his blessing on his people. John wanted his readers to grasp this concept when he wrote, "See what great love the Father has lavished on us, that we should be called children of God! And that is what we are!" (1 John 3:1). Not even the powers of hell can separate us from God's love (see Romans 8:38-39). If this is our identity—children who've been lavished upon by our Father—what will we do with what has been poured into us?

Bucket people tend to hoard what God has poured into them. Bucket people play it safe. They keep it to themselves. They refuse to take risks; they become comfortable. They live stale, predictable religious lives by attending church and other activities; and yet they miss out on the real, throbbing-with-life adventure of walking obediently in a life with Christ. Bucket people are often ungrateful, self-centered and anxious.

But pipe people give of themselves freely. They share their time, their resources, their passions, their gifts and their experiences with others regularly and frequently. They don't mind being interrupted. They proactively look for ways to pour out to others what has been poured into them. It's inspiring to watch their way of life. Pipe people are often humble, generous, faithful, joyful and infectiously grateful.

A pipe life or a bucket life—which will you be?

If I could sum up the Christian life in one word, it would be *stewardship*. God has entrusted so much to us through his grace and compassion. The book of Acts seems to be a collection of stories of people in the early church who are fully aware of God's immense blessing, powerfully and abundantly poured into their lives by the Spirit. And their heads were on a swivel just looking for people and opportunities to pass that blessing on to others.

So what are we doing with all that he's blessed us with? And what will we do with what he's blessed us with? Oftentimes, people in our church ask each other, "So, how's your pipe?" It's code language for, "How are you doing stewarding what has been entrusted to you?" Occasionally we take inventory of how we are doing as pipes. We ask, "What types of clogs have we experienced—or are we experiencing? Are the pipes getting clogged by fear or apathy, greed or sin, busyness or misaligned priorities? And what sort of plumbing work is required in order to unclog the pipe so it can flow again?"

Kingdom leaders look for and celebrate pipes in their churches. They highlight their stories. They thank God for them. They challenge others to live pipe lives. Cultivate a community of pipes—and regularly celebrate when you see pipes working as pipes should.

Church Is Free, but It Ain't Cheap!

Bob

After I had used this mantra a number of times in our gathering, encouraging people to understand the costs and economics of keeping a community running, a sign mysteriously appeared one week in front of our offering box. Someone was so taken with the saying that they decided it needed to be written up as a constant reminder to our people. It's now been in front of the offering box for years.

Most pastors have reservations and misgivings about challenging people to give. (Actually, let me rephrase that, as I wish certain high-profile television pastors had a few more misgivings about asking people to give.) *Most of us* approach talking about money and encouraging people to give with a certain level of apprehension. What I love about using this mantra is that it does the heavy lifting for me. It reminds people that they are under no obligation to put money in the box. Our church is open to anyone, regardless of how much money they have in their pockets. But we want people to understand the real costs of keeping a community going. The coffee they are enjoying (or not enjoying very much, as the case may be), the space in which we meet, paying the people who give dedicated hours to the community so they are free to do pastoral care or other work—all of these things require money to maintain.

And while money isn't *the* driving concern of our community, it is part of the overall package of life together and even spiritual growth that we want to see for people. As we've said, we encourage people to take ownership of the community, and that includes its bills and obligations. Even beyond that, we believe that the gospel, in showing us clearly the generosity of God toward us, has the effect of making us into generous people.

Whenever I use this mantra (maybe because it sounds a little pithy), I see people smile and nod as they understand its import and the implications it has on them. Without being overbearing, we remind them, "Hey, this community you love has financial needs," and we ask them boldly and unapologetically to participate in meeting those needs. It's not something we ought to be shy about as pastors, but while we want to emphasize stewardship, we certainly don't want to be heavy-handed as we do so.

You'll Be a Better Player If You Coach

Bob

While on a family vacation to Boise, Idaho, I saw a sports poster at an ice-skating rink we visited: "You'll Be a Better Player If You Coach."

I was struck by the wisdom of the statement and how it translated seamlessly to the discipleship groups in our community. The vision of our discipleship groups is that when groups are completed, people are invited to lead a group themselves. Some do, some don't and some choose to go through the group again another time. I had always lacked a clear, compelling and memorable way to challenge people to consider taking on a group of their own. I knew when I read that poster that I had found it.

One of the things I try to stress as we end our groups is that the disciplines of prayer, listening to God, living life in balance and others that we cover are not merely concepts to be learned, but skills to be practiced. People tend to do okay with them while we are doing the groups, but I suspect the tendency is to begin to forget or slowly fall back into old routines when the group is done. The challenge to continue using the skills they have learned is really the challenge to grow as disciples of Jesus.

Now I tell them that if they really want to become proficient at the skills we've talked about and practiced together, the best way is to teach and coach others in them. There's no better way to learn something than to teach others how to do it. It's okay if you feel like you are still learning yourself, but just the practice of helping others understand something leads to more mastery.

As disciples, we should all be both learners and teachers; learning from someone farther along than we are, and contributing in some positive way to someone who's not quite as far along. To me, the idea that coaching others in their walk with Jesus actually contributes to my own is compelling. All of us should be able to use Paul's famous mantra: "Follow my example, as I follow the example of Christ" (1 Corinthians 11:1). Paul told Timothy that what he had taught to him, Timothy should then teach to others who would be able to pass it along to yet more followers of Jesus (see 2 Timothy 2:2). That's *four generations of disciples* in one verse.

It may seem a bit less than altruistic to encourage people to become disciple makers by appealing to the fact that it will help themselves to be better disciples. I agree. In a perfect world, we'd all follow Jesus' call to make disciples without hesitation. That's why I appeal to self-interest only at the end of the process of making disciples. For me, it's not the sum or even the main body of the argument that they should help make disciples in our community. Rather, it's the last little push that I hope will get them over the edge to committing. Challenging the people you disciple to be more fruitful and faithful disciples by helping others is one small way to see this become a reality.

EPILOGUE

The Tomb Is Empty—the Pressure's Off

J.R.

It's all too easy to focus on what we do for God and neglect what's occurring in our inner world. If we're honest, oftentimes we work so hard *for* God that we're dry and exhausted and so God's voice seems distant.

Too often I find my work in ministry to be driven by fear and not love. *Am I doing enough? What will others think of me? Am I available to everyone the way they need me to be? Did I preach well enough on Sunday? Are we offering enough programs at our church?* This doing-religious-things-for-God mentality has often led me to feel exhausted and overwhelmed. I've stumbled into this truth: *because the tomb is empty, the pressure is off.* The good news of an empty tomb and a risen Christ is available on Easter—*and every single day after that.*

Henri Nouwen's book *In the Name of Jesus* speaks to the temptations of Christian leadership. (If you haven't read this book, read it—and if you've read it already, commit to rereading it every six months for the rest of your ministry.) The three temptations of Christian leadership—to be relevant, to be spectacular and to be powerful—can be strong and alluring. But what matters most is stewardship—how we handle faithfulness, obedience and what has been entrusted to us.

In college I served as a worship-planning assistant to Taylor University's dean of the chapel Dr. Richard Allen Farmer. I remember he concluded every email he wrote with the phrase: "Glad the tomb is empty." I was taken by this phrase. Gladness. Yes, we can be glad.

Isn't it encouraging to know that at the end of our days Jesus will never say to us, "Well done, good and successful servant"? Isn't it encouraging to know that Jesus will never say to us, "What did you do with what I didn't give you?" He will never say to us, "Why couldn't you have been like that leader over there? Why couldn't you have been as good of a preacher or singer or leader as that person over there?" In fact, God is more interested in what he is doing in and through us than how well we lead our ministries. You are not called to do great things *for* Jesus; you are called to be faithful as you are *with* God.

When my mind is buzzing with today's schedule practically spilling off the page, and my heart is anxious and burdened by all that's going on in my world, I've needed to push back from my desk, take a deep breath, exhale and whisper to myself: *The tomb is empty. The pressure is off.* It's a centering statement, getting back to this crucial truth that I had so easily forgotten.

Eugene Peterson, in his introduction to his brilliantly prophetic book *Working the Angles*, lowers the boom and focuses the issue with immense clarity:

> The biblical fact is that there are no successful churches. There are, instead, communities of sinners, gathered before God week after week in towns and villages all over the world. The Holy Spirit gathers them and does his work in them. In these communities of sinners, one of the sinners is called pastor and given a designated responsibility in the community. The pastor's responsibility is to keep the community attentive to God.[1]

When we are anxious, stressed, discouraged, overwhelmed or worried, may we remember that the pressure is off because of what happened on Easter morning.

Do not be afraid.

Do not fear.

The pressure is off.

The tomb is empty.

And for that, we can be glad.

REFLECTION QUESTIONS

1. Which two or three mantras stand out to you the most as you read the book? Why those?
2. Were there any mantras you disagreed with? Why?
3. Which mantras do you believe should be (a) remembered, (b) borrowed and repeated, (c) tweaked, (d) pondered further, and (e) ignored entirely? Why those particular ones?
4. As you've read the book, have you come to realize mantras that you may already be using in your context (but didn't know it)? Are there ways to be more purposeful and strategic in using them?
5. Are there other ministry mantras you've heard others use over the years that have shaped your own understanding or imagination about God, his kingdom, ministry or the local church? Why do you think those captured you in some way?
6. Are there mantras you've shared that may have shaped others' understanding or imagination? If so, which ones?
7. Did any new mantras come to your mind as you were reading? If so, with whom and where can those best be shared?
8. If the right mantras were used and stewarded faithfully, what impact might that have on your ministry context?
9. The fact that mantra language creates culture was discussed in the book. Are there other ways in which you could leverage language to lead and serve others, beyond just mantras?
10. Who can you process the message of this book with in order to leverage its power in ministry?
11. Does the message of this book carry any personal implications for you as you consider your leadership, approach discipleship, teach and preach, cast vision, pray for people and serve others?

ACKNOWLEDGMENTS

J.R.

Writing is a solitary act. And yet it is also deeply communal.

To our church family, The Renew Community. Thank you for embodying these mantras, living out their values and journeying with us in the little kingdom experiment called Renew.

To Doug Moister and Tracy Commons, for the roles you've played throughout the years in the leadership of our church. Thank you for your trust and friendship in this journey of ministry.

To my father, Dave Briggs, who first taught me to love language. Thank you, Dad, for showing me the power and the importance of using the right words at the right time for the right reason.

To the countless leaders I've learned from in the past—and still have the privilege of learning from today. Thank you for the wisdom, guidance and access to your life and ministry. You have left an indelible mark on my life.

And to the hungry kingdom leaders, pastors and church planters who have placed their trust in me. It is an immense privilege to invest in you. Your longing to seek God and his kingdom is inspiring.

To Andrew Wolgemuth, for your guidance and honesty. Thanks for being both professional and personal in appropriate measures.

To Al Hsu and the InterVarsity Press team, it continues to be a privilege to work with such a great group of people. Thanks for believing that this message has the potential to equip leaders for God's purposes in the local church.

To Bob, it's been an honor to work with you on this project. Thank you for bringing me in on another one of your ideas. This partnership is a privilege.

And to Christ, for not only loving and rescuing me, but also inviting me to help equip and care for your bride. All is grace.

BOB

To the people of The Evergreen Community, thank you for putting up with all the "Bob-isms" all these years. And thank you for not only putting up with them, but putting them into practice.

Thank you to Amy for believing in me more than anyone else.

Thanks to Dustin Bagby for making pastoring fun. You truly are the wind beneath my wings.

Thank you to Len Sweet, who first taught me to love a pithy turn of phrase, and showed me its power.

Thank you to Andrew Wolgemuth and Al Hsu for stewarding the dreams of regular people like me to help others through the written word.

And thanks to J.R. for letting me talk you into another project, and for all your work and care on it.

ABOUT THE AUTHORS

J.R. Briggs is the founding pastor and culture cultivator of The Renew Community, a Jesus community in the Greater Philadelphia Area. He is the founder of Kairos Partnerships, an organization that serves the church by restoring and equipping her leaders through coaching, consulting, training, writing and speaking. He is the pioneer of Epic Fail Pastors Conferences, safe and sacred spaces to help discouraged, burned out and failed pastors find hope in the midst of ministry failure. He also serves as the director of leadership and congregational formation for the Ecclesia Network.

He has written and contributed to several books, including *Fail: Finding Hope and Grace in the Midst of Ministry Failure* and *Eldership and the Mission of God*, coauthored with Bob Hyatt (both with InterVarsity Press).

J.R. and his wife, Megan, have two sons, Carter and Bennett, and live in Lansdale, Pennsylvania.

www.twitter.com/jr_briggs

www.kairospartnerships.org

www.epicfailevents.com

Bob Hyatt is the founding pastor of The Evergreen Community in Portland, Oregon. He has lived the church-planter life and knows the stresses and joys that come with it. He also finds great joy in coaching other pastors, helping them to embrace the gospel and the formation that can come through ministry. Additionally, Bob serves as the director of equipping and spiritual formation for the Ecclesia Network.

He received his Doctor of Ministry in Leadership and Spiritual Formation from George Fox Seminary and is the coauthor of *Eldership and the Mission of God* with J.R. Briggs.

Bob loves reading and spending time with his wonderful family—his wife, Amy, and their children, Jack, Jane and Josie.

www.twitter.com/bobhyatt

www.bobhyatt.me

www.ecclesianet.org

NOTES

FOREWORD

[1]Nelson Goodman, *Ways of WorldMaking* (Indianapolis: Hackett, 1978).

[2]Robert Adams, *Along Some Rivers: Photographs and Conversations* (New York: Aperture, 2006).

INTRODUCTION

[1]Guy Kawasaki, "Don't Write a Mission Statement, Write a Mantra" (talk presented at Stanford University's Entrepreneurship Corner, July 1, 2011), www.youtube.com/watch?v=2A2-7_nujtA.

[2]Michael Pollan. *Food Rules: An Eater's Manual* (New York: Penguin, 2009), xv.

[3]Ibid.

[4]Marshall Goldsmith and Mark Reiter, *What Got You Here Won't Get You There: How Successful People Become Even More Successful* (New York: Hachette, 2007), 145.

[5]From the title of John Burke's book, *No Perfect People Allowed: Creating a Come-as-You-Are Culture in the Church* (Grand Rapids: Zondervan, 2007).

[6]From a personal conversation with Eugene Peterson (Lakeside, MT: June 2010).

[7]An alteration of a quotation from Erwin Raphael McManus, *An Unstoppable Force: Daring to Become the Church God Had in Mind* (Elgin, IL: David C. Cook, 2001), 176.

[8]From Rick Warren, *The Purpose Driven Church* (Grand Rapids: Zondervan, 1995), 32.

STRUCTURE MUST ALWAYS SUBMIT TO SPIRIT

[1]Erwin McManus, *An Unstoppable Force: Daring to Become the Church That God Had in Mind* (Colorado Springs, CO: David C. Cook, 2013), 77.

[2]J.R. Briggs and Bob Hyatt, *Eldership and the Mission of God* (Downers Grove, IL: InterVarsity Press, 2015), 54-55.

[3]For another helpful metaphor, see Colin Marshall and Tony Payne, *The Trellis and the Vine: The Ministry Mind-Shift That Changes Everything* (Kingsford, NSW: Matthias Media, 2009).

BET THE FARM ON DISCIPLESHIP

[1]Alan Hirsch, *The Forgotten Ways: Reactivating the Missional Church* (Grand Rapids: Brazos Press, 2009), 10.

[2]Neil Cole, *Search & Rescue: Becoming a Disciple Who Makes a Difference* (Grand Rapids: Baker Books, 2008), 185.

EVERY CHURCH IS BORN PREGNANT

[1]Bill Easum and Thomas G. Bandy, *Growing Spiritual Redwoods* (Nashville: Abingdon Press, 1997), 184-203.

GOD USES CRAZY PEOPLE TO SEE THE KINGDOM EXPANDED

[1]The Ecclesia Network is a relational network of mission-oriented churches seeking to partner, equip and multiply other churches on mission. Both of our churches are members of this tribe, and both of us have the privilege of serving on staff part-time. For more information on the Ecclesia Network, see www.ecclesianet.org.

[2]One of the four principles in the book *Surfing the Edge of Chaos: The Laws of Nature and the New Laws of Business*, by Richard T. Pascale, Mark Millemann and Linda Gioja (New York: Crown Business, 2001).

DON'T TRY TO MAKE CHURCH RELEVANT TO THE CROWDS; MAKE THE GOSPEL RELATABLE TO THE CONTEXT

[1]For more on "third places," see sociologist Ran Oldenburg's *The Great Good Place: Cafes, Coffee Shops, Bookstores, Bars, Hair Salons, and Other Hangouts at the Heart of a Community* (Washington, DC: Marlowe & Co., 1999).

[2]Alan Hirsch and Michael Frost, *The Shaping of Things to Come: Innovation and Mission for the 21st-Century Church* (Peabody, MA: Henrickson Publishing, 2003), 113.

NO MATTER WHAT, GIVE HOPE

[1]For more information, see our initiative at www.epicfailevents.com and J.R.'s book *Fail: Finding Hope and Grace in the Midst of Ministry Failure* (Downers Grove, IL: InterVarsity Press, 2014).

[2]John Ortberg, "The Barnacles of Life: What Dallas Willard Taught Me about Living the Jesus Way in Ministry," *Leadership Journal*, Winter 2015, 55.

IF THEY KNOW YOU LOVE THEM, YOU CAN SAY ANYTHING TO THEM

[1]Richard Baxter, *A Call to the Unconverted to Turn and Live* (1658).

PUSH—BUT DON'T SHOVE

[1]The components of lightweight, low maintenance and high accountability have been used by others to describe missional communities. We find that these elements and values are so important that we implement them into almost every structure we have. We see these values played out throughout the Scriptures quite frequently.

MINISTRY IS MEETING PEOPLE WHERE THEY ARE AND JOURNEYING WITH THEM TO WHERE GOD WANTS THEM TO BE

[1]Graham Cray in his opening plenary talk at the Fresh Expressions US National Gathering on March 16, 2012, at First Baptist Church in Alexandria, VA. For more on Fresh Expressions, see www.freshexpressionsus.org.

THE ESSENCE OF DISCIPLESHIP IS NOT KNOWLEDGE, BUT IMITATION

[1]Dallas Willard, "How Does a Disciple Live?," *Radix* 34, no. 3 (Spring 2009), available at www.dwillard.org/articles/artview.asp?artID=103.

REMEMBER, THE VEGETABLES AREN'T READY YET

[1]Eugene H. Peterson, *A Long Obedience in the Same Direction: Discipleship in an Instant Society* (Downers Grove, IL: InterVarsity Press, 2000), 17.

PAY ATTENTION TO GOD, AND RESPOND APPROPRIATELY

[1]Eugene Peterson, *Working the Angles: The Shape of Pastoral Integrity* (Grand Rapids: Eerdmans, 1987), 2.

ASK THE RIGHT QUESTIONS AT THE RIGHT TIME TO THE RIGHT PEOPLE FOR THE RIGHT REASON

[1]For more on the questions Jesus asked and answered, see John Dear's *The Questions of Jesus* (New York: Doubleday, 2004); Eric Burtness's *Lenten Journey: Beyond Question* (Minneapolis: Augsburg Fortress, 2012); and Martin B. Copenhaver's *Jesus Is the Question* (Nashville: Abingdon Press, 2014).

IF YOU WANT TO SEE GOD, LOOK FOR RED JEEPS

[1]Lawrence Kushner, *Eyes Remade for Wonder: A Lawrence Kushner Reader* (Woodstock, VT: Jewish Lights, 1998), 10-11, emphasis added.

[2]Elizabeth Barrett Browning, "Aurora Leigh," in *The Oxford Book of English Mystical Verse*, ed. D. H. S. Nicholson and A. H. E. Lee (Oxford: Clarendon Press, 1917), 86.

CARE MORE ABOUT SENDING CAPACITY THAN SEATING CAPACITY

[1]This idea was first shared by Reggie McNeal in a plenary session at the Fresh Expressions US National Gathering on March 16, 2012, at First Baptist Church in Alexandria, VA.

SLAY THE BEAST OF AMBITION BEFORE IT SLAYS YOU

[1]Dallas Willard, "New Age of Ancient Christian Spirituality (A)," Q & A transcribed by Scott Sevier, *Steadfast* editor (July 18, 2002), available at http://dwillard.org/articles/artview.asp?artID=95.

[2]A. J. Swoboda shared this during a plenary session at the Ecclesia National Gathering on March 10, 2016, at Eastpoint Community Church, in Newark, DE.

LET YOUR CALENDAR SAY NO

[1]Eugene Peterson, *The Contemplative Pastor* (Grand Rapids: Eerdmans, 1989), Kindle edition, loc. 206.

[2]Will Willimon, *Pastor* (Nashville: Abingdon Press, 2002), 36.

THE WORLD NEEDS MORE WELL-RESTED LEADERS

[1]Bill Clinton, quoted in Greg McKeown, *Essentialism: The Disciplined Pursuit of Less* (New York: Crown Business: 2014), 95.

[2]For more on rest as a spiritual practice, see James Bryan Smith, "What Are You Seeking?" in *The Good and Beautiful God: Falling in Love with the God Jesus Knows*, The Apprentice Series (Downers Grove, IL: InterVarsity Press, 2009).

THE ONLY THING YOU SHOULD BE ANXIOUS ABOUT IS HAVING A NONANXIOUS PRESENCE

[1]For more on "self-differentiated leaders," see Edwin Friedman, *A Failure of Nerve: Leadership in the Age of Quick Fix* (New York: Seabury Books, 2007); or Jim Herrington, Robert Creech and Trisha L. Taylor, *The*

Leader's Journey: Accepting the Call to Personal and Congregational Transformation (San Francisco: Jossey-Bass, 2003).

WE WILL LET YOU DOWN: IF WE'RE CLOSE ENOUGH TO HELP, WE'RE CLOSE ENOUGH TO HURT

[1]Along these lines, Dietrich Bonhoeffer wrote this in *Life Together*: "By sheer grace, God will not permit us to live even for a brief period in a dream world. He does not abandon us to those rapturous experiences and lofty moods that come over us like a dream. God is not a God of emotions but the God of truth. Only that fellowship which faces such disillusionment, with all its unhappy and ugly aspects, begins to be what it should be in God's sight, begins to grasp in faith the promise that is given to it. The sooner this shock of disillusionment comes to an individual and to a community the better for both." Dietrich Bonhoeffer, *Life Together: The Classic Exploration of Faith in Community* (New York: HarperOne, 1978), 11.

WHEN WE PUT ON OUR MASKS, WE PUT ASIDE THE CROSS

[1]This chapter is adapted from J.R. Briggs, "Loneliness: The Temptation to Wear Our Masks," in *Fail: Finding Hope and Grace in the Midst of Ministry Failure* (Downers Grove, IL: InterVarsity Press, 2014).

[2]See Jerry Bridges, *Respectable Sins: Confronting the Sins We Tolerate* (Colorado Springs, CO: NavPress, 2007).

[3]For a more in-depth look at masks, see Russell Willingham, *Relational Masks: Removing the Barriers That Keep Us Apart* (Downers Grove, IL: InterVarsity Press, 2004).

[4]Madeleine L'Engle, *A Stone for a Pillow*, Genesis Trilogy (London: Shaw Books, 2000), 94.

[5]Dallas Willard, "Becoming the Kinds of Leaders Who Can Do the Job," *Cutting Edge*, Summer 1999, available at www.dwillard.org/articles/artview.asp?artID=165.

[6]N. T. Wright, *Paul for Everyone: Galatians and Thessalonians*, The New Testament for Everyone (Louisville, KY: Westminster John Knox Press, 2004), 23.

COME AS YOU ARE, BUT DON'T STAY AS YOU ARE

[1]We learned of this from John Burke's book by that title: *No Perfect People Allowed.*

[2]Dietrich Bonhoeffer, *The Cost of Discipleship* (New York: Touchstone, 1995), 217.

IT'S NOT COMMUNITY UNTIL IT GETS HARD

[1]Dietrich Bonhoeffer, *Life Together* (New York: HarperOne, 1978), 11.

EVERYTHING IS FORMATION

[1]Eugene Peterson, *The Pastor* (New York: HarperCollins, 2001), Kindle loc. 144.

FEW THINGS MESS WITH YOUR THEOLOGY MORE THAN READING YOUR BIBLE

[1]Dorothy L. Sayers, *Letters to a Diminished Church: Passionate Arguments for the Relevance of Christian Doctrine* (Nashville: Thomas Nelson, 2004), 4.

[2]See Scot McKnight, *The Blue Parakeet: Rethinking How You Read the Bible* (Grand Rapids: Zondervan, 2008).

DISAGREE WITHOUT DISENGAGING

[1]John Wesley, quoted in Christian T. Collins Winn, Christopher Gehrz, G. William Carlson and Eric Holst, eds., *The Pietist Impulse in Christianity* (Cambridge: James Clarke and Co. 2012), 329.

BE MISSIONARIES CLEVERLY DISGUISED AS GOOD NEIGHBORS

[1]John Quick, July 23, 2013, https://twitter.com/John_Quick/status/359722041768820738.

[2]J. D. Greear, *Gaining by Losing: Why the Future Belongs to Churches That Send* (Grand Rapids, Zondervan: 2015), 95.

BELONG BEFORE YOU BELIEVE

[1]Rick Richardson, *Reimagining Evangelism: Inviting Friends on a Spiritual Journey* (Downers Grove, IL: InterVarsity Press, 2006), 27.

BE A PIPE, NOT A BUCKET

[1]I first heard this analogy used by Matt Heard, former senior pastor of Woodmen Valley Chapel (Colorado Springs, CO) in 2002.

EPILOGUE

[1]Eugene Peterson, *Working the Angles: The Shape of Pastoral Integrity* (Grand Rapids: Eerdmans, 1987), 2.